WHEN
THE FUND
STOPS

Every owner of a physical copy of this edition of

WHEN THE FUND STOPS

can download the eBook for free direct from us at Harriman House, in a DRM-free format that can be read on any eReader, tablet or smartphone.

Simply head to:

ebooks.harriman-house.com/whenthefundstops

to get your copy now.

WHEN THE FUND STOPS

The untold story behind the downfall of Neil Woodford, Britain's most successful fund manager

David Ricketts

HARRIMAN HOUSE LTD
3 Viceroy Court
Bedford Road
Petersfield
Hampshire
GU32 3LJ
GREAT BRITAIN
Tel: +44 (0)1730 233870

Email: enquiries@harriman-house.com
Website: harriman.house

First published in 2021.

Paperback ISBN: 978-0-85719-865-5
eBook ISBN: 978-0-85719-866-2

British Library Cataloguing in Publication Data
A CIP catalogue record for this book can be obtained from the British Library.

Harriman House

For Tara, Orla and Daniel

CONTENTS

"I'll be here for decades to come. My best years as a fund manager are still in front of me."

– Neil Woodford, 2014[1]

PROLOGUE

Dazed and Confused

Two hours' notice

NEIL WOODFORD was about to have the worst possible start to his week.

At around 6am on 3 June 2019, the renowned UK fund manager arrived at the headquarters of his eponymous investment empire located on a drab business park on Garsington Road, about a ten-minute drive from the centre of Oxford.

After completing the hour's journey from his home in the Cotswolds and parking his top-of-the-range black Audi, the stocky 59-year-old walked a few short steps to the entrance of the three-storey glass-fronted building, unaware that his day would take a dramatic turn several hours later.

Woodford, once the poster-boy of the British investment management industry, had a lot on his mind that morning. He had spent the weekend fretting that one of his biggest clients

1

was about to walk away from his ailing flagship investment fund. But he was not prepared for the development to come, which would leave his career and status as one of Britain's most revered investors hanging in the balance.

At its peak two years previously, the Woodford Equity Income fund had been the best-selling investment product in the UK, and had grown assets to more than £10bn. A horde of individual savers and heavy-hitting investors had piled into the fund having followed Woodford closely for more than two decades. Equity Income's launch in June 2014 was the most successful in British history. Hundreds of thousands of regular investors wanted a piece of the action and pumped vast sums of money into Woodford's fund after it was lauded by the financial press, online investment platforms and seasoned market pundits.

After just one year, Equity Income was a strong performer, returning 17.9% and comfortably beating the market and sector benchmarks.[2] Delivering stellar returns, investors continued to flood into Woodford's blockbuster fund. Woodford's track record spoke for itself and his success over a career spanning almost three decades helped him amass a huge fanbase. He was treated like a rock star and had the lifestyle to boot, owning a fleet of sports cars and a sprawling country estate complete with stables to satisfy his love of horse riding.

Once dubbed "the man who can't stop making money", an initial investment of £10,000 with Woodford in 1988 during his time at Invesco Perpetual, a large US-headquartered investment manager, would have grown to £309,000 if investors had stuck with him throughout the first year of his new venture.[3] His career even earned the royal seal of approval, with Woodford awarded a CBE in the 2013 Queen's birthday honours for services to the economy. He picked up his gong from Prince William at a lavish Buckingham Palace ceremony.

On paper, Woodford had the track record and accolades any investor would find hard to ignore. But five years after leaving Invesco Perpetual to establish Woodford Investment Management, the tide had well and truly turned for Britain's answer to legendary US investor Warren Buffett. A series of bets on companies which then endured a succession of profit warnings put a severe dampener on his performance, prompting hordes of jittery retail investors to cut their losses and make a swift exit. By June 2019, it appeared that Woodford had lost his Midas touch. Assets in his biggest fund had more than halved from its pinnacle, to just £3.7bn.

The majority of clients still stuck by Woodford, convinced he could turn around his run of poor performance. He was under immense pressure to reassure remaining investors that he had his most successful fund under control. But matters were about to get a lot worse.

Kent County Council was one of Woodford's biggest investors. It had £240m sitting in the Equity Income fund on behalf of more than 100,000 pension scheme members. The council had a long association with Woodford, stretching back to his heyday as a star fund manager at Invesco Perpetual. Like a loyal friend, it had stayed with him through this bout of poor performance. But that loyalty had now, it seemed, been tested too far.

In the months leading up to 3 June, Woodford's largest fund was bombarded with requests from investors to pull their money. Facing a rising wave of redemptions, the embattled fund manager was having to offload shares in some of his largest holdings to raise the hundreds of millions of pounds he needed each month to pay investors back. The size of the withdrawals were staggering and picking up pace, but so far Woodford maintained a grip and was managing to keep up. Investors pulled slightly more than £100m from the fund during the first six months of 2017, but this ballooned to almost £1.5bn over the same period the following year, according to figures from Morningstar, a company which tracks investor money entering and leaving investment funds.

The situation began to spiral as Woodford sold stakes in some of the biggest and highest-quality companies to pay back investors wanting to get out, meaning some of the unquoted holdings became more prominent within the fund. As investors continued to walk, the fund reached a crisis point as cash needed to be raised from some of these harder-to-sell assets.

It was not just ordinary savers who were starting to abandon Woodford. City investors with hundreds of millions of pounds tied up with the fund manager were also losing faith. Jupiter Fund Management, a large London-based asset manager, had withdrawn its £300m investment in the Equity Income fund towards the end of 2017, ending a 20-year relationship it had with Woodford. Aviva, the UK insurance giant, had also ditched the fund manager during the same year and reclaimed £30m.

Woodford was losing some of his most high-profile clients at an alarming rate. Kent County Council had also lost patience, having seen the value of its investment plummet by almost £80m over a two-year period.[4]

Like the thousands of ordinary savers who had already walked away, the Maidstone-headquartered council was about to serve its notice on Woodford. Little did they or Woodford anticipate the chain of events that would follow their bombshell announcement.

On the afternoon of Friday 31 May, Woodford's team was told by Nick Vickers, head of financial services at Kent County Council, that the local authority's pension fund committee members wanted to pull its investment. There were options available to Kent. One would be to stagger its exit from the fund over several months, a move which would give Woodford breathing space to keep up with mounting outflow requests from other investors. The pension fund could also choose an 'in-specie transfer', meaning assets in the fund could have been transferred to Kent County Council to match the size of its investment, negating the need for Woodford to sell any of his holdings to raise cash.

Woodford's team were preparing themselves for the difficult break-up talk at a meeting they had scheduled with Kent

County Council on 21 June. But the meeting would never take place.

On the morning of 3 June, Woodford's team – including compliance head Chris Martin, chief executive Craig Newman and head of IT Paul Green – gathered in the boardroom to prepare for a routine conference call with Link Fund Solutions, the company responsible for the oversight and administration of Woodford's Equity Income fund. Representatives from Northern Trust, the US-headquartered bank which acted as the safekeeper of investor assets in Woodford's largest fund, were also on the line. The phone call came through at 9.30am. The voice of Karl Midl, Link's managing director, filled the room. Woodford's team and Link talked through the various ways to manage Kent's impending exit, but it was a futile exercise.

During the course of the call, official confirmation came through that Kent County Council wanted to pull its *entire* holding in the Equity Income fund and that the money was to be redeemed immediately. The decision was final.

Woodford was about to be dealt an even more devastating blow. Following a meeting of Link's board at 11am, the decision was taken to suspend the Equity Income fund. The Financial Conduct Authority would be informed of the decision at 11.30 – just two hours after Woodford and Link had begun their conference call to discuss how to manage Kent County Council's impending exit.

Woodford's team were caught off guard by Link's decision to suspend the fund. It was not the course of action they were expecting. A hurried statement to explain the decision to journalists was drafted and Woodford's team prepared themselves for the incoming media frenzy. Link's official statement issued that afternoon claimed the suspension was in the best interests of investors, and the move would allow Woodford time to reposition his portfolio to more liquid stocks.

The Equity Income fund, which invested in mainstream companies such as house builders Taylor Wimpey and Barratt Developments, also had a large allocation to companies that were not publicly traded on the stock market or where holdings would take longer for Woodford to sell. Link told investors the decision to suspend the fund would be reviewed in 28 days. But their words provided little reassurance to stunned investors who now found themselves trapped in the fund, unable to access their savings.

———

Paul McInerney was on the phone with his brother on 3 June 2019 when he received news that the Woodford Equity Income fund had been suspended, locking in £28,000 he had invested. Like thousands of other individual investors, the former financial services professional from Kent had used Hargreaves Lansdown, one of the UK's largest online investment platforms which had heavily championed the fund from its launch.

McInerney was among a large cohort of investors who followed Woodford during his illustrious career at Invesco Perpetual. Woodford's winning streak was enough for

McInerney to follow the fund manager when he parted ways with Invesco to set up his own fund management company.

"When I heard he was leaving to set up on his own, at that time he could almost do no wrong. He was the golden boy," says McInerney. "A bit like if a football manager wins the FA cup with one team and moves to another, you get the feeling they'll do well somewhere else."

But it soon became clear to McInerney that Woodford was not generating the kind of stellar returns he had done during his days under his old employer. The 50-year-old, who invested in the Woodford Equity Income fund via his self-invested personal pension and individual savings account, had kept a close eye on its performance in the year leading up to the suspension, after it became clear performance was beginning to stutter. Rather than cut his losses, McInerney continued to stick with Woodford – convinced he could reverse his losing streak. He was also reassured by the fact that Hargreaves Lansdown continued to promote Equity Income on its Wealth 150 list – the platform's best pick of investment funds, backed by its internal research.

"I was still optimistic even though people were pulling money out. I was thinking 'let's give him more time'," says McInerney. News of the fund suspension came as a complete shock. "My initial thought was: how long will it be frozen? I knew some of the assets were less liquid, so I wondered when I might get my money back."

McInerney's story echoes those told by countless other savers who had invested money with Woodford in good faith after he received glowing endorsements from Hargreaves Lansdown. Denise Geary entrusted £38,000 to Woodford's fund when it first launched and was also caught out by news of its suspension. The 63-year-old had chosen the fund after diligently carrying out her own background research into Woodford and seeing Equity Income prominently placed on Hargreaves Lansdown's recommended list of funds. "He seemed to have good credentials and did well at Invesco. He was highly regarded. It's why I invested in his fund," says the clinical research worker from Manchester.

Geary's investment initially paid off, with her investment at one point reaching £46,000 with Woodford's early performance. But her high opinion of the fund manager quickly reversed after the value of her original investment nosedived. "I thought this is what markets do and it will recover. I thought I can't pull out now because I'll lose a lot of money and it'll improve. Before I knew where I was, it was frozen," says Geary.

Geary, who had set the money aside to pay for an extension on her home, was forced to take out a bank loan and borrow from a family member to fund the work. "I'm very angry about it," she says. "Woodford was arrogant. He didn't waive his fat fee. He has got to be held to account."

———

Woodford's Equity Income fund never did re-open following its suspension in June 2019.

Instead, the decision to freeze the fund kick-started a catastrophic chain of events that would eventually bring the curtain down on the career of one of Britain's most renowned stock pickers and rock the investment sector to its core.

Woodford's spectacular downfall was inconceivable when he left Invesco Perpetual in 2014 at the top of his game. The widely held belief was that, having been unleashed from the constraints of a large corporation, Britain's best-performing fund manager would be free to flourish in his own organisation, investing on his own terms. But he failed to live up to the high expectations and his business imploded in the most spectacular fashion.

The events of 2019 have cast an unfavourable light on the investment platforms and financial pundits who continued to champion Woodford, despite concerns emerging about how his largest fund was being managed and when the warning signs started to appear two years previously.

The full impact of Woodford's downfall is still being felt today, and it will go down in history as one of the biggest fund management scandals in Britain. The question investors are now asking is: will it be the last?

This book tells the story of the astonishing rise and fall of Neil Woodford – a man who won the trust and savings of millions of ordinary people before losing both in the most dramatic fashion possible. Pieces of this drama have been told before in the press; this book, for the first time, goes deeper – revealing many new, unexpected and sometimes disturbing aspects of a saga still sending shockwaves through the world of finance.

It is the tale of how the one-time hero of fund management

turned villain, continuing to rake in millions of pounds in fees from investors who were left stranded in his biggest and best-selling fund. It is also the story of how the financial watchdog, which should have the best interests of investors at its core, failed to act on the warning signs and rein in one of Britain's most powerful fund managers and those responsible for the oversight of his multi-billion pound fund.

But most of all it is a tale of how one man, who had built up a vast personal wealth on the back of his investment prowess, believed too much in his own hype – and eventually paid the ultimate price.

I

Good Times, Bad Times

The young Woody

I

IT had always felt like his destiny, but now he could practically touch the clouds. Years of after-school training and boyhood dreams had brought him to this place. But more than that: it was in his blood. His father had taken to the skies during the second world war and lived to tell the tale. And those tales had lit a fire inside a young Neil Woodford.

That fire had finally propelled him to RAF Biggin Hill, a defunct fighter station sitting atop the North Downs in Kent, once proud home to Spitfires (a full-size replica, rather than a statue of a saint, stands outside its chapel) but now more accustomed to the buzz of light leisure aircraft.

Woodford had been a member of the Maidenhead 155

Squadron of the Air Training Corps for several years at this point. Twice a week, the teenager had attended its meetings, held in a wooden hut with a corrugated roof, which also doubled as a base for the Jehovah Witnesses and local scout group. Aside from fostering an interest in an RAF career, young cadets undertook activities such as shooting, hovercraft building and gliding. One meeting involved Cadet Woodford being strapped into a fighter jet's ejector seat.

Now the well-built sixth-former – his hair a thick rug of brown curls above his trademark rugby-flattened ears – sat and awaited his results.

This was no formal application to join the Royal Air Force. To get to that, you had to get past this: a series of aptitude tests, assessments designed to give aspiring aviators an indication of whether they even had the basic skills to become fully-fledged trainee pilots. Members of the air training corps had also been given the opportunity to apply for valuable flying scholarships, meaning the RAF could pay for these school leavers to study for their private pilot licence during their summer holidays.

Woodford had visited with four other members of the Maidenhead squadron. Now the results were in. It was good news for some – in fact, better than good; four of the squadron had secured scholarships.

One hadn't. The clouds suddenly seemed further away than ever for Woodford. He had passed the navigation test. But the results for the pilot aptitude test were another matter. The main problem, he is told, are his reaction speeds. They're just not fast enough.[5]

Born in the upmarket Berkshire village of Cookham on 2 March 1960, Neil Russell Woodford was the second child to hairdresser Pamela and publishing and printing business owner Victor. Situated on the banks of the Thames, Cookham during the 1960s was considered a quintessential English village, best known for its association with British painter Stanley Spencer, who was born there in 1891.

Woodford's parents were married on 27 September 1952 at St Laurence church in Slough, and their first son, Simon, was born six years later.[6] Despite growing up in a well-to-do area, Woodford and his family were by no means wealthy. "Things were tight, but we got on", said Woodford in an interview with *The Times* in 2015.[7]

Living in a three-bedroom semi-detached house overlooking Westwood Green in Cookham, the Woodfords played an active role in their village community. Neil and his brother featured in a 1971 production of *The Spider Monkey Uncle King* – a children's opera commissioned by the Cookham Festival Society, which told the story of how the wise old king of a faraway land is overthrown by a young imposter, who fools everyone by being able to transform into a spider and monkey. Neil played one half of a set of twins and Simon took on a choral role.[8]

Woodford was gifted academically and had no problems with his schoolwork. After attending the Holy Trinity Church of England Primary School in Cookham, he passed the 11-plus exam and joined an intake of 150 boys at nearby Maidenhead Grammar School in September 1971. The school was overseen by headmaster L. C. Reynolds, who was affectionately known as 'Elsie' to his pupils. Reynolds, who was also a local magistrate and chief scout, was a strict disciplinarian and expected nothing but the very best of the Maidenhead boys. "My contention is that excellence is to be found in personal and corporate performance at every age and every level of ability and that it is totally right to see it at all those levels," he said at one annual school speech day.[9]

The school, which later became known as Desborough College, counts Woodford among an illustrious list of past pupils. *Dragons' Den* star Peter Jones, author Nick Hornby and *Phantom of the Opera* lyricist Charles Hart are all 'Old Maidonians'. Woodford, known as 'Woody' to his classmates, was in the same year as Guy Fletcher, who went on to play keyboard for Dire Straits (Woodford is a self-confessed Eric Clapton and Led Zeppelin fan).

Maidenhead pupils were sorted into five classes during their first year, with boys grouped according to their surnames. Woodford was identified as a high achiever almost immediately, and in his second year was placed in the 'A Stream', where he was pushed to achieve the best possible grades. A popular boy, eager to learn, Woodford was an ideal pupil in many ways. In his fifth year was awarded the Parents' Association prize for all-round contribution to school life.

Away from his schoolbooks, Woodford excelled in sports, particularly rugby (which he continues to follow to this day with a passion). He played centre forward for the school's 1st XI hockey team. Woodford was also a performer when it came to individual events. Strong shoulders, a fast arm and explosive speed over short distances made him a natural javelin thrower. He would later go on to become the Berkshire schools javelin champion in the late 1970s – an achievement which made him eligible for the All England Athletics Championship.

Woodford's first job while at school was cleaning machinery in a Beecham's factory, located in nearby Maidenhead.[10] But his big aspiration had been a career in aviation. With his childhood dream of flying crushed, Woodford instead embarked on a completely different career path. Removing his head from the clouds, he looked towards the soil, and went to study agricultural economics at Exeter University.

By the time he graduated from Exeter in 1981, unemployment in Britain had risen to its worst level since the 1930s and rising levels of discontent and poverty sparked riots up and down the country, notably in Liverpool's Toxteth and Brixton in London. After sleeping on the floor of his brother's flat in London, Woodford got his experience in the world of finance when he scored a job as an admin clerk at a commodities merchant – a job which gave him zero satisfaction. ("It was unbelievably boring and tedious," he would later recall.[11])

Woodford's first proper money management role came when he landed a job at the Dominion Insurance Company in 1981, working as an assistant to fund manager Bill Seddon. Seddon, who went on to become chairman of the insurance firm, remembers Woodford as a conscientious trainee, whose remit was to learn the basics of company analysis and to develop a nose for a good investment. It would prove to be Woodford's first steps on the road to a career in fund management.

With Seddon responsible for overseeing the Dominion's entire investment portfolio, the post allowed Woodford to gain a good grounding in managing exposure to cash, bonds and equities. There were few obvious signs of fund management flare, though. "To be honest, I didn't think 'My goodness, this is the next Warren Buffett'," says Seddon. "He did what he was asked to do. If I wasn't around, he coped."

After just over two years at Dominion, Woodford moved to the Reed pension fund as a UK equities analyst, applying the knowledge he had built up working alongside Seddon. By the mid-1980s, Woodford had started to cut his teeth in the City, which itself was on the cusp of immense change. Margaret Thatcher was about to wave in an unprecedented programme of deregulation designed to help London compete more effectively with the world's other major financial centres, in what would be known as Big Bang. But it was Woodford's move to the Trustees Savings Bank, an institution which began as a local savings bank in Dumfriesshire, that would prove to be one of his most memorable career moves.

II

There was the interview and then there was the Test. Impressing at the former was no mean feat; this was an ambitious firm. But it wasn't much good if you failed the latter. Unfortunately, what made the Test especially difficult was that interviewees never knew they were being subjected to it. And they only ever got one attempt.

Neil Woodford was 25 years old and sitting in the reception of the Trustee Savings Bank on Milk Street in the heart of the City of London, waiting to be interviewed. It was 1986 and most offices in the UK were characterised by a quality almost no one at the time would have noticed and which today almost no one would believe. Smoking at your desk was freely allowed and widely practised. Behind the windows of the offices on Cheapside and Moorgate and London Wall, the air was misty with clouds of Dunhill, Rothmans, Camel and dozens of other tobacco brands Woodford would later make millions investing other people's money in.

Behind the windows of the Trustee Savings Bank, however, things were different. The directors operated an unspoken policy. But an unspoken policy could only be effective if enforced by other means.

That means was the Test.

A bubbly 30-year-old woman from East London approaches the young Woodford. He doesn't know it but she's the personal assistant to Ian Marshall, head of the strategic planning unit where Woodford has applied for a junior analyst post. She will be something even more important soon. Her name is Jo Mullan. She greets him. Woodford is relaxed – and wonderfully polite. His confidence and manners leave a mark. Later, it's the main thing Jo remembers of their first meeting.

Woodford is asked if he will require an ash tray during the interview. Without much thought, he declines. The manners were important – in a moment, Jo will, unseen by Woodford, give a thumbs-up signal to the interviewer, who has no time for haughty applicants and likes to remind his assistant: "If they are rude to you, I need to know." But accepting or declining the ash tray was the Test. And Neil Woodford has passed it.

The smoke-averse senior managers of TSB have managed once again to find out if they risk hiring someone who would be tempted to light up in the office, a habit they cannot stand but which they find awkward to discourage. They are also about to give one of the most profitable tobacco investors in history his first big break.

———————

Woodford goes on to impress Marshall in the interview, pipping the other candidate to the job. It is up to Jo to deliver the good news. She had returned to work at the bank only six months previously, having undergone several years of gruelling surgery and chemotherapy to tackle an extremely rare form of cancer, which had almost cost her life.

She put in a phone call to Woodford late on a Friday afternoon before heading home from the office. "Ian said he would do a letter to offer Neil the job, but I suggested we should phone him instead," says Jo. "I thought it would make his weekend. He was over the moon."

When Woodford arrived to start his new job, TSB was on the verge of a major transformation. It had listed on the stock market in 1986 and had raised around £1.2bn from the flotation, breaking previous listing records in the City of London.[12] It was at TSB that Woodford truly acquired the research and analysis skills he would carry with him throughout his career as a fund manager. Unlike building societies, where any money raised from a listing would be returned to depositors, TSB got to keep the cash. With more than £1bn at its disposal, TSB sought to buy companies it could then add to its line-up and help expand. Working in a small department of about 20 staff, Woodford's job was to scrutinise potential acquisition targets and rate them based on two metrics: their attractiveness and whether they would be a good fit for the bank. "He was very easy to deal with – and the perfect person for the role," recalls Marshall.

Marshall left TSB not long after the stock market listing to work in advertising, but kept in touch with Woodford. The two later met for lunch in a cafe outside the Barbican in 1987. Woodford had grown concerned. He had serious reservations about the bank's acquisition of Hill Samuel, the merchant bank for which it had recently submitted a bid.

Woodford had developed a good eye for spotting dud companies and he had a bad feeling about this particular acquisition. He told Marshall that, according to his own analysis, Hill Samuel was neither an attractive proposition nor a good fit for TSB. He certainly did not think it was worth the more than £700m that TSB was willing to pay, a sum that would leave a huge dent in the money it had raised during the flotation. But as a junior analyst, Woodford was powerless. Venting to Marshall didn't change anything. The deal was pushed through.

Woodford and Jo often found themselves working late in the Milk Street office long after their colleagues had gone home.

The two had hit it off immediately when Woodford arrived for his job interview. Now it didn't take long before they forged a closer relationship. "He was a popular guy and worked very hard. He was very fun-loving and we had a lot of common interests," says Jo.

While the relationship remained professional during the first few months working together, an affectionate message sent to Jo from Woodford in a birthday card revealed he was interested in taking their friendship further. It couldn't have come at a better time for Jo. "I had just had cancer and I wasn't happy in my marriage at that time. We had met when I was 15 and it was never going to work. We were more like brother and sister living together and it was just a question of who was going to meet someone first. I met Neil and decided to leave. I told my husband to find someone he loved."

The relationship developed quickly over the next year and the couple moved into a house in Knowsley Close in Maidenhead. Marriage was on the cards, but the proposal did not go as Woodford had planned. Thanks to nosy neighbouring diners at a romantic meal out, he ended up having to ask Jo to marry him in a shop doorway a few yards down from the restaurant. She immediately said yes.

The couple were married in Maidenhead Registry Office on 18 September 1987. It was an intimate wedding, attended only by the bride and groom's fathers and a handful of other guests. The wedding reception took place at the couple's suburban home.

In the years before Jo and Woodford met, his parents'

marriage had fizzled out. They had fallen out over Victor's decision to hand over his publishing and printing business to someone in the family for next to nothing – something Pamela never forgave him for. The couple later divorced, but found love again with new partners. Victor married a woman he had met while walking his dog and later moved to Worcester, while Pamela married her childhood sweetheart.

Woodford kept in touch with his parents until their respective deaths, but his brother Simon became estranged. Victor died on 14 February 2015, splitting his entire £850,000 estate between Neil and other benefactors, including the RAF and several animal welfare charities. Simon was left nothing. In his will, his father said that he had not spoken to his son for more than 20 years.[13]

———

Four years after Woodford's marriage, and his lunch with Marshall, Hill Samuel was about to meet an unfortunate milestone. The firm Woodford had urged his employer not to buy had been on a lending spree. By 1991 it had attained the dubious achievement of amassing more than £500m worth of bad loans on its balance sheet.[14] It was a huge amount – and it plunged TSB into a loss for the year. Woodford was vindicated at last. "He was absolutely right," recalls Marshall. "Hill Samuel brought TSB to its knees." But by that point Woodford had moved onto bigger things. And there was no one around to see him proved right.

2

If it Keeps on Raining

The overnight millionaire

I

I T was well outside office hours when an unfamiliar car pulled up outside a dark building in the heart of a quiet Oxfordshire town. The wind and rain were beating down. Two figures sat inside the vehicle, its headlights on and engine still running. Neither of them would have been familiar to anyone watching. But, for now, at least, they seemed to be unobserved. That was good, because the hour was late and their business was urgent.

Abruptly, one figure slips out into the storm, carrying something in one hand – shielding it from the wet as he approaches the building. Inside sits a very modern business, but the structure that contains it could be something out of a German fairy tale.

Then, a second later, it's over.

The damp letter drops to the ground inside the empty office, and the figure turns about and makes for the car, the windscreen wipers beating off the rain and the leaves like flailing arms.

Neil Woodford has just applied for the job that will make his name.

They say no story should start with a dark and stormy night, but sometimes they just do. Woodford had been sitting at home in Maidenhead earlier that windblown evening in 1988 when he decided he wanted a change. Not long after he had expressed concerns to Marshall about TSB's purchase of Hill Samuel, Woodford had moved to insurance company Eagle Star to take up a fund manager post. He had been at Eagle Star for less than a year, but the daily commute to the City was taking its toll. His wife Jo had given up commuting to work in the City and wanted to concentrate on starting a family. She needed less stress and had secured a personal assistant job a short drive from their suburban home. But with only one car between them, Woodford was taking the coach to work in London. The arrangement was far from ideal.

A solution came when Woodford heard about Perpetual, a fast-growing asset management company based in nearby Henley-on-Thames which had recently listed on the stock market. Woodford was drawn to its proximity and what sounded like a unique culture. As the rain pelted down outside, Woodford made a few changes to his CV and drafted a speculative application.

But he was impatient. Instead of dropping his letter in the post, that evening Woodford and his wife drove the short distance to Perpetual's head office – all decorative gables and timber frames on historic Hart Street in Henley – and popped the envelope through the front door.

Opening the newspaper the next day, Woodford spotted a job advert for Perpetual. His timing couldn't have been better, but he was worried the letter he had just hand delivered might arouse suspicion that he had been tipped off about upcoming jobs. Woodford set about penning another application with the hope it would make his unprompted first attempt appear less suspicious.

Perpetual management never said if they had suspected anything – or if they had been bemused by the strangely timed double application. Woodford's efforts paid off. He joined the company in early 1988.

———

Perpetual was set up by flamboyant British businessman and racehorse owner Martyn Arbib in 1974. Born in June 1939 and educated at the prestigious public Felstead School in Essex, the sharp-dressed, bouffant grey-haired business executive began his career as an accountant at Spicer and Pegler.

Like the Queen – with whose hair Arbib's has always borne a striking resemblance – he had a fondness for horse racing.

However, Arbib denied being a serious gambler – even if he possessed an enviable winning streak. A series of bets he placed at a meeting in Newmarket in 1962 won him £3,000 – a sum large enough in those days to fund a two-year trip to Australia.[15]

On returning to the UK, Arbib shifted his focus to investing in the stock market. It came as little surprise to those that knew him that bookmaker Ladbroke, which had recently floated in London, piqued his interest. According to Arbib, the company possessed three key strengths which made it worthy of his investment: solid management; an expanding business; and positive cash flow.

Backing Ladbroke proved the right move for Arbib, and he made the decision to pursue stock picking full time. He went on to set up Perpetual in 1974, starting the business in Henley with just one office in Hart Street and overseeing £5m in assets. After the company listed on the stock market in 1987, Arbib and his family retained a 45% stake. Arbib maintained his passion for horse racing and set aside £250,000 from the money he got from floating Perpetual to invest in horses – naming his first Snurge, after a nickname he had earned at school. Snurge proved another successful investment for Arbib, winning the St Leger at Doncaster in 1990. It also held the record for collecting the most prize money of any European-trained horse, around £1.3m over a 34-race career.[16]

A characteristic of Arbib's – soon a defining feature of Woodford, too – was his staunch belief that there were advantages to be had in managing money away from the

City. Arbib believed keeping fund managers away from the distractions of brokers and analysts in London allowed them to fully focus on delivering results. "Perpetual had an anti-establishment whiff about it," says one former employee. "The investment guys were not from the Oxbridge draw and enjoyed not being part of the establishment and not being distracted by the City. Henley is a bit like that. It's a remarkably inaccessible place. That was all part of the culture."

As Perpetual flourished, it forged a reputation as one of Henley's major employers. Rapid expansion meant it soon outgrew its Hart Street office and several others dotted about the town. Perpetual Park was then opened in 1997.

On joining Perpetual, Woodford was initially put in charge of overseeing the High Income fund, with his own Income fund launched two years later. Perpetual proved popular among investors in personal equity plans – a tax-efficient predecessor to individual savings accounts (or ISAs) – and Woodford's fund was soon demonstrating an ability to attract investors due to his strong performance.

By the mid-1990s, Perpetual was one of the best-known fund management brands in the UK, thanks to its aggressive advertising campaigns. The company was firing on all cylinders and had made a fortune for Arbib. The *Sunday Times* Rich List showed he had increased his personal wealth by £133m in 1993 alone following a bumper year of sales for the company.[17] Woodford was also riding the wave of success. The Perpetual High Income fund had been a consistent top performer since its launch. By the end of 1994 it had amassed around £500m in assets.

Woodford was managing to impress not only Arbib but also a legion of financial advisers who were keen to recommend the fund manager to their clients. But one of Woodford's most challenging periods was about to come.

II

It wasn't the most pleasant way to start a Sunday. A lazy morning in bed with breakfast and the weekend papers should have been ideal. But Woodford, turning through that day's *Sunday Times*, found his morning ruined – to say nothing of his appetite.

Someone was calling his professional judgement into question. And not just any pundit: they were from Hargreaves Lansdown, a growing brokerage firm in Bristol that had recently launched its own investment platform with ambitions to become the "Tesco of the retail investment world".[18] It was a rare rebuke from a firm who would later be his biggest cheerleader – and many of whose customers' financial fates would become intertwined with his business.

"Woodford has an excellent 12-year track record so you cannot write him off," said Hargreaves Lansdown's Alan Durrant in a *Sunday Times* article from January 2000. "But I am not convinced that his decision to avoid telecommunications and pure technology stocks is right."

It was not the first time Woodford had felt the pressure of late. In the bucolic riverside town of Henley, with its ornate Georgian townhouses and Tudor coffee shops, you could sometimes forget the 20th century. But the world was changing

– and fast. People brought it home from newsagents, on shiny discs sellotaped to glossy magazines: the Internet.

AOL, Compuserve, Prodigy and other internet companies – with a little help from British Telecom – had been connecting the world's computers like never before. Suddenly, anything seemed possible. You no longer had to set foot inside a bookshop to pick up the latest best-selling novel. You could even summon pizza to your door from your videogames console.[19] Fortunes were being made overnight, in strange speculative businesses with names like Excite, Flooz, Gadzoox and Amazon. They came out of nowhere – and often made paper millionaires of their founders and any lucky early investors.

But one man was not convinced. Woodford refused to follow the herd. The turn of the millennium saw the dotcom fever rise to a pitch; still he remained unmoved. And his reluctance to get involved had not gone unnoticed. His wisdom was being called into doubt – and Durrant was far from the only dissenting voice.

Woodford had enjoyed tremendous sales and performance success during his time at Perpetual. But the performance of his blockbuster High Income was waning. Other investors couldn't pile into technology stocks fast enough. Woodford, meanwhile, had stayed loyal to the big names that had delivered solid returns, such as cigarette giants Imperial Tobacco and British American Tobacco – old-fashioned companies that were, at least, profitable and paid dividends. The problem was their price movements were just not as sensational as those companies caught up in the dotcom bubble. The result looked like underperformance.

Woodford had grown assets in the High Income fund to almost £2.5bn by the start of 2000. Now people were wondering if the party might be coming to an abrupt end. Arbib was even breathing down Woodford's neck to make sure Perpetual got a piece of the action. "Martyn was really testing Neil," says one former Perpetual employee who worked with both men. "He saw not being involved in some of the tech stocks as a business risk. Some people would say Neil was stubborn, but he was self-assured. I wouldn't say he was arrogant – not at that stage."

As companies like Microsoft, Amazon and AOL continued to fuel the dotcom boom, the Nasdaq reached an all-time high on 10 March 2000, having registered 16 new highs during the first ten weeks of the new millennium. Woodford failed to win over his doubters. An article in the *Mail on Sunday* that same month carried a survey of 14 leading independent financial advisers. Twelve said they would not recommend Woodford's High Income fund, given that its performance was now the worst compared to others in its peer group. "Woodford is a good manager, but maybe his pride is getting in the way," said Alan Penney, one of the financial advisers quoted in the *Mail on Sunday* article.[20] "He is becoming more intransigent."

In the UK, stock prices continued to go through the roof. Shares in online travel company lastminute.com rocketed from 380p to 511p in the first hour of trading on 14 March 2000, valuing the company at £768m. The celebration was short lived. By the end of the company's first day on the stock exchange, shares had fallen below their offer price.[21] They eventually fell to 150p in the first month of trading. The boom was well and truly over.

The collapse of a string of technology companies shortly thereafter meant Woodford was soon vindicated. This time he was still in place to see it – and to bask in the glory.

————————

Woodford's defiance on holding technology companies paid off and he was richly rewarded when it came to Arbib setting his remuneration. "Martyn awarded him something that made him a millionaire overnight," says Jo Woodford, who remembers celebrating with her husband with a drink after Arbib had called.

Woodford's newly acquired millionaire status brought with it a dramatic change in lifestyle. One of his first big purchases was Fingest Manor, a grade-II listed property in Henley so vast it required a team of grounds staff. There was also the purchase of a second home in Devon, a favourite destination for Woodford who had enjoyed family holidays there as a child.

Woodford had a large garage built at Fingest Manor to store the Ferraris for which he had started to develop an affection. His obsession with fast cars led to him racing at the Goodyear Maranello Ferrari Challenge in Northern Italy, his blue and yellow F355 model sporting the 'Woody' nickname he acquired as a schoolboy.

He was a thrill seeker when he got behind the wheel. "When it was wet people would slow down, but not Neil. The crowd would be so excited. He did have a few crashes and caught fire once," recalls Jo.

By the middle of 2000, Perpetual had grown to around 400 staff and assets under management had swelled to £13bn. Rumours began to surface that Arbib was looking to sell the business. In May of that year, Perpetual confirmed it was engaged in talks over a deal, but Arbib remained tight lipped about the identity of any potential suitors. In October it was announced that US-headquartered Amvescap had sealed the deal and would pay £1bn – creating Britain's second largest fund management group after Fidelity. Arbib pocketed around £450m. There were sweeteners for top fund managers, including Woodford, to prevent any immediate defections. Losing Woodford was a crisis Perpetual's new owners were keen to avert.

III

Shortly after the deal was completed, talks began about how Perpetual employees would be brought together with Amvescap's European fund management operation, Invesco, which was based in London. The discussions led to anxiety among Perpetual's Henley-based fund managers, who had grown accustomed to the lifestyle away from the City of London. Suggestions of moving to London were immediately shot down by Woodford. He made his thoughts on the matter known to his new bosses. Moving out of Henley was not an option.

"Henley was seen as the jewel in the crown of the Invesco business. Fund managers like Neil were regarded as demigods and treated like football stars," says one former Perpetual employee who worked in Henley alongside Woodford. "There was a sense that whatever Neil asks for, Neil gets."

Perpetual staff were able to stay put in Henley and Arbib was kept on in an advisory role. Arbib's close ties with the local council as one of Henley's largest employers allowed him to protect the Perpetual Drive name he had chosen for the road leading up to the office, ensuring he left a lasting mark for years to come after the Amvescap deal.

Mergers can create uncertainty and questions began to emerge about Woodford's future at the firm, as well as other top-performing managers such as Stephen Whittaker, who managed the UK Growth Fund. Like Woodford, Whittaker was regarded as one of Perpetual's star performers. He had also avoided being caught out by the dotcom crash in 2000, having steered clear of technology stocks. Woodford pledged his allegiance to Perpetual's new owners by signing a five-year contract. Whittaker, meanwhile, defected to New Star, a fund management company set up by City veteran John Duffield.

Although Whittaker left Perpetual with an admirable track record, there was a sense that he and several other fund managers in Henley were living in Woodford's shadow and struggling to make their own mark. "The problem with the UK department of Perpetual was when you looked at the portfolios of other fund managers, they were in the same sectors as Neil," says one former colleague of Woodford and Whittaker. "If you were on the UK fund management desk and you made a bet different to Neil and it didn't work out, that was uncomfortable."

Woodford had averted one crisis by resisting pressure to invest in technology companies towards the end of the 1990s. But he would achieve another major feat by dodging the catastrophic fallout from the 2008 financial crisis. "He went into the banking crisis with no banks. That's hugely impressive," says a former colleague who worked closely with the fund manager at Henley. "He got dotcom right and then he got banks right. The whole culture of Woodford as a star manager was reinforced."

Ten years on from Perpetual's tie-up with Amvescap, Woodford had forged his reputation as one of Britain's best-performing stock pickers, earning himself the nickname the 'Oracle of Oxford' as comparisons began to be drawn with veteran US investor Warren Buffett (often dubbed the 'Oracle of Omaha').

Such was his stellar reputation, it was not uncommon to see the bosses of some of the UK's largest companies being summoned to meet Woodford in his Henley office. Chief executives knew how important it was to keep on the right side of Woodford.

One of the first company bosses who fell out with Woodford was AstraZeneca's David Brennan. The pharmaceutical giant was one of Woodford's largest holdings in his High Income and Income funds. But by 2012, profits and revenues were sliding under Brennan's watch and the company was failing to produce enough new drugs to keep up with the competition. Brennan received a £9m pay package in 2011 and top shareholders, including Woodford, were vying for change. On 26 April 2012, just hours before AstraZeneca's annual shareholder meeting, Brennan announced his retirement.[22] The company denied they had ousted Brennan, but Woodford's criticism of the way he was running the company was widely seen as a contributing factor to his departure.

Less than a year later Woodford was jostling for another change at the top – this time at Eddie Stobart. Woodford's funds owned almost 40% of the road haulage company. But with a profit warning issued after shares had fallen by more than 20% in a year, Eddie Stobart's long-standing chairman Rodney Baker-Bates was given the boot. Woodford threw his support behind Avril Palmer-Baunack, who was appointed as executive chairman with the task of selling off underperforming parts of the company. "There has been a need for a change in leadership on the board and Avril fits that role perfectly," Woodford said at the time.[23]

Orchestrating the removal of Brennan and Baker-Bates had been done largely behind the scenes, but Woodford was not always so clandestine. In October 2012, he went public about his opposition to a planned merger between UK defence company BAE Systems and EADS, a civil aerospace group now known as Airbus. Invesco, via Woodford's High Income and Income funds, owned around 13% of BAE Systems. A planned €38bn deal between the two companies promised to create an aerospace giant, but Woodford, who had held shares in BAE at various stages for more than 20 years, was concerned that planned cost reductions and synergies would not be enough to deliver significant value to shareholders. There was also a political element to the deal that needed to be considered. The British government retained a 'golden share' in BAE after it sold off its holding in the 1980s, meaning it could veto the possibility of foreign ownership. And the French and German governments would have needed to approve a deal involving EADS.

Woodford's status as a hard-hitting and influential investor meant he was able to summon chief executives to Henley at short notice, rather than face the inconvenience of travelling to company headquarters himself. BAE Systems chief executive Ian King was called to Henley for a heated meeting that lasted several hours, in which Woodford laid out his concerns about the tie-up.[24] He was not a fund manager company bosses wanted to get on the wrong side of. Woodford made sure company executives like King took notice of him. Other shareholders voiced similar concerns about the potential merger and were counting on Woodford to give King a rough ride on their behalf. "Neil looks like an SAS soldier rather than a fund manager," one analyst at a rival fund manager said at the time. "You wouldn't want to fight him verbally or physically."[25]

Ultimately, political differences proved too difficult for BAE and EADS to overcome. The merger finally failed after Germany voiced strong opposition.

One of Woodford's boldest investment decisions came in April 2012 when he sold his entire holding in Tesco, arguing the food retailer needed to spend less and focus more on shareholder returns. Woodford's funds had held Tesco stock for 20 years, during which time it had proved a very successful investment. But the fund manager was convinced he could deploy the money raised from offloading his Tesco stake to bolster some of his existing holdings, as well as hunting for cheaper stocks with less risk.

Woodford's increasing interest in stewardship – engaging with companies on behalf of shareholders – set him apart from other fund managers at the time, who were on the receiving end of criticism for not having a keen enough interest in what was happening in company boardrooms.

Woodford was a key contributor to the landmark Kay Review in 2012, a study of UK equity markets and long-term decision making authored by prominent economist John Kay. Woodford was particularly critical of how fund performance was consistently measured over short time periods and the industry's "obsession" with demanding companies publish financial reports every quarter. He was also damning on pay structures implemented across fund management companies, arguing that they tended to be weighted towards rewarding performance over a one-year period rather than longer time frames.

When the Review was finally published, Woodford modestly claimed: "I am an exception in the industry." He went on: "I take corporate engagement very seriously. The industry is failing on this point, but it is possible ... to accept responsibility of ownership."[26]

As Woodford's career was going from strength to strength at Invesco, the same could not be said about his marriage.

IV

Neil and Jo Woodford were walking their German shepherd dogs in woods close to their Henley home early one Sunday morning in March 2007. It would be a walk Jo would never forget. "I knew something was wrong," she says. "I kept saying 'You seem troubled. Why can't you talk to me?'"

Out of nowhere, Neil told Jo that he wanted a divorce.

Jo had noticed a change in her husband's behaviour in the months leading up to his bombshell announcement. He had become more distant and irritable. A recent trip to Australia to attend a wedding had been a particularly uncomfortable experience. "I couldn't do anything right. We had a lot of arguments. It was not a happy time."

Their morning walk in the woods took place three months after returning from their overseas trip. Neil broke the news that he had been having an affair with his secretary, Madelaine White. "He said they had already got a flat," says Jo. "I ran away from him all the way to the house. What was upsetting was that it had all been done and put in place. I was completely floored. My heart ached."

During 20 years of marriage, the Woodfords never fulfilled their dream to have children, despite multiple attempts. Jo suffered several miscarriages and gave birth to a stillborn baby boy, which would be their final try at starting a family. "I was almost there, but I was 39 and decided I couldn't do it anymore," says Jo. Accepting the cards they had been dealt, the Woodfords developed a passion for animals. This led to them rescuing a handful of Dartmoor ponies near their Devon home. Woodford also took part in a swim to raise funds for the conservation of the white rhinoceros.

Woodford's high profile meant he was often approached for help. One unusual request came from the owners of a Siberian tiger called Tessa, who had gained notoriety after featuring in a well-known Esso TV advertising campaign during the 1990s. In 1998, a dispute had erupted between North Wiltshire District Council and Kington Langley Wild Animal Centre, where Tessa was housed, over the planning permission needed to keep dangerous wild animals.[27] Esso had pledged £25,000 to help find Tessa a permanent new home, but Woodford was approached to see if he could add to the coffers. Despite visiting Tessa – one of Jo's biggest regrets is not entering the enclosure with her – Woodford did not pledge any financial help.

Nevertheless, Woodford demonstrated generosity by helping the grandson of a family friend born with intestinal problems – donating funds to a local hospital so he could receive treatment locally, rather than travelling hundreds of miles to a specialist treatment unit.

The Woodfords' separation was far from plain sailing. While the divorce was still being completed, Neil and Madelaine moved into a small gamekeeper's cottage on the grounds of

Fingest Manor, where Jo was still living. "They lived there for almost a year. I had to pass them every day. I was disappointed with Neil that he let that happen," says Jo.

Despite their marriage ending abruptly, Neil and Jo remained amicable during the divorce proceedings, even when it came to sorting through possessions at their Henley home. "When the van arrived to take away the furniture, the drivers must have thought it would be awful and that there would be arguments. But it wasn't like that at all. We kept in touch for several years after our divorce," says Jo.

Jo, who remarried in August 2019, was among those investors with money tied up in Woodford's Equity Income fund. Her financial adviser suggested she pull her investment from the fund about a year before it was suspended. Instead she chose to stick by her ex-husband. "I had so much faith in him," she says. "I thought he could turn it around and put it right. I've personally lost a lot of money. I don't feel sorry for myself – but I do for others who have lost a lot of their pension savings."

3

Whole Lotta Love

The star breaks free

I

THE UK sales team at Invesco Perpetual could sense something was not right. It was a regular morning towards the end of May 2013 but their boss, Craig Newman, was nowhere to be seen.

Newman stood out. A cocksure, straight-talking redhead, he had quickly climbed the ladder to become Invesco Perpetual's sales director, overseeing the team responsible for promoting Woodford's funds. He was described by one former colleague as running the sales team "with fear and vision". Now he had disappeared. For a man who liked to be both seen and heard, it was strange to say the least.

Simon Dale, Newman's right-hand man and head of retail

sales, was also missing in action. Invesco Perpetual's senior management were silent over their whereabouts. It made the situation a tricky one to manage for those remaining members on the sales desk. Two new colleagues had joined the team earlier in the week, and it was becoming increasingly difficult for those who already worked alongside Newman and Dale to conjure up new excuses to explain their absence. Of course, it was not uncommon for both Newman and Dale to be out of the office together. Both would spend time on the road attending client meetings, and Newman was known for coming into the office later than most of the senior team. But this felt different.

One personal assistant who worked alongside Newman and Dale, and who was known to share office gossip, was silent. Her reluctance to spill the beans was a dead giveaway to the rest of the sales team that something more serious was going on.

"The initial uncertainty was bizarre," says one former Invesco Perpetual employee who was in the office that day. "People were talking about what could have happened. Nobody really knew. But people were starting to wonder if it was a wider crisis."

Ian Trevers, who oversaw distribution in Henley, informed the sales team there were no more details senior management could divulge about the departures, only that he would be taking over Newman's position until a replacement was found in the new year. "While management wouldn't comment on the specifics of the situation, they were keen to make sure the sales team was reassured and kept motivated," says the former sales employee.

It didn't take long for rumours to sweep the office about why Newman had made a sudden exit, with now ex-colleagues speculating he had been dismissed for downloading client data. Newman says his resignation from Invesco Perpetual was subject to a confidentiality agreement and has always denied any wrongdoing.

It was an abrupt and ignominious-looking end to a successful 17-year career with Invesco Perpetual.

"People are usually only marched to the front door for a fairly short list of reasons. It was very unglamorous and a huge shock," says another former Invesco Perpetual employee who worked with Newman.

The UK team was filled with people with unconventional backgrounds. This suited Woodford, who himself eschewed the City and was regarded as an outsider. One of the sales team was Ross Lamacraft, who had worked in regional sales at supermarket chain Lidl before joining Invesco Perpetual in 2006 as a business development manager. Before that he spent two years as an RAF pilot.

To those working in other roles at the Henley office, the UK team was a "boys club", with those working directly under Woodford and members of the sales desk often socialising together.

Newman was a challenging boss and got results, but he was not easy to approach. "He was like a male lion − impressive from afar but you would not want to get too close," says one of his former colleagues. "Craig spent a remarkable amount of time not in the office," adds another. "But he delivered fantastic sales growth. While Neil was delivering, it was easy for the sales team."

Fitness fanatic Woodford, who had spearheaded the introduction of an onsite gym at the Henley office, could often be found working out during his lunch break alongside some of his sales colleagues. "Neil dominated the weights room and the punch bag, often shouting at the wall," says one former employee. "You'd see Neil and his team working out together and going back to their desks pumped. It was a macho culture that didn't include everyone."

At the time of Newman's departure, Woodford remained dominant within the Henley operation – but he was becoming increasingly cut off from the rest of the office. He had ordered a partitioned office to be built, with a sofa and conference call facilities to separate him from the rest of his team. It was a space for Woodford to work uninterrupted – and he became increasingly difficult to approach directly. There was a growing sense the fund manager was unhappy. There were frequent outbursts. "Neil could lose his temper – and was seen to do that with management as much as with his own team," according to one former colleague.

Those working in the Henley office sensed a source tension was a changing of the guard among the senior leadership. Bob Yerbury, who had been chief investment officer of Invesco Perpetual since 2008, retired in 2010 after more than a quarter of a century in Henley, including as its UK CEO. A deep-thinking Cambridge maths graduate, Yerbury was part of the Perpetual old guard, having been brought in by Arbib in the

1980s to run its US investment team. Yerbury was replaced as CIO by Nick Mustoe, a no-nonsense manager described by one former colleague as "a karate black belt who was tough and free of emotion". Like Woodford, Mustoe was obsessed with keeping fit and would spend time working out in the office gym.

Mustoe's management style was in complete contrast to Yerbury's. Woodford found himself facing questions about his investment decisions. "It's fair to say Bob had been a light-touch manager," says a former colleague who worked with Yerbury and Mustoe. "He was interested in investments, but his management was quite benevolent and not testing. When Bob retired and was replaced by Nick, that's when Neil was called to account in a way he hadn't been before."

Woodford had started to develop an appetite for smaller companies offering higher growth potential. This marked a departure from his holdings in safe, well-established stocks that had driven much of his past success. It wasn't long before his investments in companies outside his usual realm caught the attention of his superiors in Henley. Concerned about the heightened level of risk management needed to invest in private companies, Mustoe set up a more formal risk management group in 2012, reporting directly to him, which was designed to keep a close eye on Woodford's activities. The new arrangement did not go down well with Woodford.

"At the same time Neil was looking for new ways to walk on water, the risk control element was tightening up," says a former colleague. "Telling Neil he couldn't do something was a red rag to a bull. The relationship between Neil and Nick was bristly."

With Newman out of the picture, and sensing Woodford was becoming unsettled, Mustoe started to accelerate other changes in Henley. He needed to prepare for the eventuality that their top performer would walk at any moment. Invesco's management were confident they could rely on their star fixed income managers, Paul Causer and Paul Reed, but Woodford's funds had grown to such a size that his departure could put the business on extremely shaky ground. The solution was to poach a line-up of more top-performing fund managers from Edinburgh-based rival asset manager Standard Life Investments. David Millar, Dave Jubb and Richard Batty arrived to join the Henley team in early 2013.

The trio had worked on a popular strategy called the Global Absolute Return Strategies fund, another blockbuster investment product in the UK with around £12bn in assets at the time their appointments were announced. It was a major coup for Mustoe. "It felt like they needed to make a bold move, knowing that Neil was agitating," says a former Invesco Perpetual staff member.

Mustoe and the internal committee set up to keep a close watch on Woodford were not the only ones interested in the levels of risk being taken on by Invesco's funds. The Financial Conduct Authority had also begun to ask questions about the amount of leverage being introduced into some of Invesco's products. It started to probe whether savers were being properly informed about the risks. Its investigation found that between May 2008 and November 2012 investors in 15 Invesco funds had been exposed to higher levels of risk than they had been led to expect on 33 separate occasions.[28]

The FCA said the losses from taking on excessive risk amounted to £5m, which Invesco paid back into the funds by way of compensation. Two of the funds identified by the regulator were the High Income and Income funds overseen by Woodford. One of the funds, Managed Income, was run by Mustoe. The investigation ended with Invesco being slapped with an £18.6m fine. The timing of the announcement by the regulator turned out to be unfortunate for Woodford – published a month before he was due to unveil his first fund at a new venture.

II

Invesco Perpetual staff were arriving at the Henley office on 15 October 2013 when an email dropped into their inboxes which got their immediate attention. The message, topped with a headshot of Woodford, announced their biggest star was leaving. It caught everyone in Henley off guard.

Invesco Perpetual CEO Mark Armour outlined how Woodford would step down from the business the following April, and referenced vague plans about him setting up his own venture at a later date. The internal memo also detailed how Mark Barnett – Woodford's protégé – would be elevated to head of UK equities, replacing Woodford in one of the most important roles in the business. Barnett would also take over management responsibilities on the Income and High Income funds, giving him control of around £33bn, including the

Edinburgh Investment Trust (an investment mandate outside of Invesco which Woodford also ran).

The amount of money now under Barnett's control was staggering. It represented a huge chunk of Invesco Perpetual's overall assets, which were around £70bn at the time. The departure was sobering for both Invesco and Barnett, who knew it was only a matter of time before investors would walk out and follow Woodford to his new business. Financial pundits predicted that billions would flow out the door.

Barnett, who ran the Strategic Income fund at Invesco Perpetual and three other funds, had worked alongside Woodford for 17 years and was regarded as the obvious choice to take the reins. He was also keen to stress the similarities he shared with his mentor. At the time he took over from Woodford, six of the top ten stocks owned by High Income and Barnett's Strategic Income funds were the same. A change in fund manager was not going to lead to a dramatic change in investment style. "We talk an awful lot about stocks," Barnett said in an interview shortly after Woodford announced his departure. "We take account of macroeconomic considerations when we take a view. Our largest holdings are quite similar."[29]

Darius McDermott, a seasoned financial commentator from Chelsea Financial Services, was on a corporate golf day when news broke of Woodford's unexpected exit. He was in the clubhouse when he became inundated with phone calls from financial journalists eager to get his take on the biggest personal finance story of the year. "To me it was the biggest fund management news of the decade," says McDermott.

Comparisons were soon made between Woodford's exit and other well-known fund managers who had recently made surprise departures from their organisations. One unavoidable example was Anthony Bolton, the veteran investor at Fidelity International. Bolton, a classical music composer in his spare time, first retired from managing money in 2007. But he was coaxed out of retirement in 2010 to move to Hong Kong and manage a new China-focused portfolio. Several months before Woodford's departure announcement, Bolton said he would retire for good, having failed to deliver the stellar returns he was renowned for during his City career.

Like Woodford, Bolton was lauded for his ability to consistently invest in winning companies. Investors didn't have much cause for complaint, having seen £1,000 invested in his Fidelity Special Situations fund grow into more than £148,000 over the 28 years he managed it. But replicating his UK success in his China Special Situations trust proved too difficult for Bolton, who conceded he had struggled. "The most disappointing thing for me – and I am happy to admit it – is that I was wrong about the market in China," Bolton said in an interview just before his departure from Fidelity. "I thought it would go up for four years but it has gone down over four years."[30]

Woodford's departure was also compared to that of Richard Buxton, another member of the City stock-picking elite who managed almost £4bn of investor money at Schroders, the listed UK fund management company. After an 11-year stint, Buxton announced in March 2013 that he was leaving Schroders for

Old Mutual Global Investors. Predictions that Schroders would suffer significant outflows on the back of Buxton's departure were correct. In the year that followed, investors pulled almost half the assets from the UK Alpha fund Buxton had overseen, while money continued to follow him through the door at this new employer.[31]

Woodford's departure eclipsed all of these.

"It was the high profile of Neil and the size of assets he was running which made it such big news," says McDermott. Invesco's share price dropped 5% on the announcement, wiping hundreds of millions from the company's value in one fell swoop. Armour moved swiftly to offer reassurance to shareholders, saying the company had "planned for succession for many years" and that it had a "well-ordered transition process" in place.

Woodford said that he would remain "fully committed" to his fund management responsibilities until his departure, but in reality staff were already adapting to a new era under Barnett. Some were relieved an increasingly agitated Woodford had made the decision to leave. "Neil essentially left the day his departure was announced," says one former Invesco Perpetual employee. "There was a sense that with Neil gone, the boil had been lanced. While there would be outflows, it was time to rebuild under Mark."

Barnett may have been considered a safe bet, but the task ahead of him was huge. With loyal investors keen to follow Woodford, outflows from the High Income and Income funds soon began to mount. In the two months following Woodford's departure, investors pulled £1.3bn. And the outflows only escalated: over the first six months of 2014, leading up to the launch of Woodford's maiden fund, the funds bled almost £4.2bn.[32]

"Following Neil was something of a poisoned chalice because of his track record, his stature and the amount of assets he was running" says McDermott. "Almost entirely from the second Mark took over, he would have been selling stocks to fund redemptions."

III

By the time Woodford had gone public with his plans to leave Invesco Perpetual, his former colleague Newman had already been laying the groundwork for the new venture the pair would eventually run together. Newman had formed a close relationship in the time he had worked with Woodford and spotted an opportunity for the pair to strike out on their own, free from some of the overbearing risk management controls that had been put in place at Invesco Perpetual under the change of CIO leadership.

Woodford's desire was to remain distant from the big fund management giants in the City of London. In addition, to satisfy most of the former Invesco Perpetual investment team who he would later poach from Henley, it was agreed the new operation would be located on a business park in Oxfordshire. The nearest pub was a Beefeater attached to a Premier Inn across the road from the office, while Harley Davidson's UK base was on the opposite side of the roundabout.

It was an unglamorous spot for a start-up that would be investing billions of pounds in some of the UK's largest companies. But it was also convenient for Woodford, who lived about an hour away on a farm in Tetbury with his former secretary, who he went on to marry in 2015 and with whom he had two children.

Their home, built on land which the couple bought for £13.7m in 2013, was a short drive from Highgrove House, the country retreat owned by the Prince of Wales.[33] The couple had moved to the area situated in the Cotswolds after falling out with neighbours in Skirmett, near Henley-on-Thames, over a planning application in 2011. Woodford's new wife was an equestrian fanatic, and her passion for amateur showjumping had rubbed off on her husband, who by now was showing more interest in horses than in his Ferraris. The couple had planned to build a vast all-weather equestrian centre on Valentine Farm, comprising a riding arena, stables, tack rooms, feed and rug room, wash rooms, office and store rooms.

Jeremy Paxman, the former BBC *Newsnight* presenter, was one of those local residents outraged by the plans and the potential impact on the local countryside. Paxman, who lived in the neighbouring village of Stonor and was renowned for not mincing his words, wrote to Wycombe District Council to vent his frustration, calling the proposed development "enormous, unsightly, inappropriate and environmentally unfriendly". He wrote: "We are told in the application that it is a 'private' development of a mere 28 stables and rooms, along with an arena … In the context of Chiltern villages, this is like describing Wembley Arena as a 'private' development."[34]

Nigel Starmer-Smith, the former England rugby international, was also among other famous locals who objected to the Woodfords' plans. One resident even went as far as to suggest that redevelopment of the property, once owned by Formula 1 tycoon Flavio Briatore, resembled a prison camp. Following protests from locals, the Woodfords withdrew their application. Wycombe District Council refused planning permission on a second attempt lodged a year later.

Fortunately for Woodford, applying for the necessary permissions to get his new business up and running were more straightforward. Woodford Investment Management received regulatory approval from the FCA extremely quickly, considering that Woodford and Newman were setting up an investment management outfit from scratch and were expecting to run money for a large number of retail investors. The application was submitted to the regulator in January; the business was authorised in April.

The wheels were now in motion. But Woodford still needed support to get his new business up and running. Assistance came from Peter Dubens, an intensely media-shy internet entrepreneur and founder of Oakley Capital, a London-based private equity firm which has a large stake in listings magazine *Time Out*. The stout, foppishly haired Dubens founded Oakley Capital in 2007 and had a track record of growing start-ups, including 365 Media Group, which he sold to BSkyB for more than £100m, and internet service provider Pipex, which was later acquired by Tiscali for more than £200m.[35]

Dubens and Woodford knew each other well, and the High Income and Income funds both held investments in Oakley Capital. Oakley announced in December 2013 that it would be providing the infrastructure to enable Woodford to start managing money the moment he left Invesco Perpetual. The arrangement was more of a gentleman's agreement rather than anything formal.

Woodford soon began to assemble a team consisting of those he most trusted, making a slew of hires from Invesco Perpetual. Stephen Lamacraft, who was a pan-European equity manager based in Henley, joined Woodford's investment team as a fund manager. His brother Paul, another hire from Invesco Perpetual, joined as an analyst. Saku Saha, another defector from Henley who had focused on assessing some of the smaller companies Woodford had started to take an interest in, was also drafted in.

The list of business heads soon grew to resemble a group of close mates. The other Lamacraft brother, Ross, joined Woodford's new sales team from Invesco Perpetual, alongside Simon Dale whose new role was to oversee the retail sales element of the business. William Deer, who had been with Invesco Perpetual since 2006, took on the role of pitching for institutional mandates. Mitchell Fraser-Jones also joined from Invesco Perpetual to head up investment communications.

Paul Farrow, a former personal finance hack at the *Daily Telegraph*, was one of the few outsiders hired by Woodford. Farrow had moved from his job at the *Telegraph* to work at high-end bank Coutts to lead its communications, and would do the same for Woodford. Gray Smith, a lawyer from Mishcon de Reya who had helped shepherd Woodford through the FCA investigation at Invesco Perpetual, was hired as chief legal and compliance officer and would become one of the main partners in the firm. Another outsider was Nick Hamilton, who was installed as one of the senior leaders of the business, having worked at Invesco Perpetual as head of global equity product. He had moved to Australia after ten years with Invesco Perpetual to work with Colonial First State. But after just six months in the job he was enticed back to the UK by Woodford's offer.

The arrangement was for Woodford to own 65% of the venture while Newman, who assumed the role of chief executive, held the remaining 35%. It was a business set-up that would prove extremely lucrative for the duo, who would later pocket tens of millions of pounds in profits.

Despite being described as the "driving force" behind Woodford Investment Management on the company's website, Newman had little experience running a business and zero money management expertise. "Craig, who had no investment management experience at all, owned a third of the business. How on earth did that come about?" says one of Newman's former colleagues from Invesco Perpetual. "It is intriguing how strongly Neil must have been influenced by Craig."

4

Stairway to Heaven

The £5bn launch

I

IT wasn't every day you could relax with a £20 glass of champagne beside a London double-decker bus parked amid palm trees and cotton awnings as crisp and bright as yacht sails, but then it wasn't every day you successfully launched a fund management firm that thousands of people couldn't wait to invest in.

Neil Woodford's new team hadn't actually travelled to a tropical island by bus. They'd arrived at the Crazy Bear, a quirky and faintly decadent hotel complex set within 80 acres of working farmland in Stadhampton, Oxfordshire, in a fleet of taxis and high-spec cars. The vintage Piccadilly bus – decked out with neon signage and a solitary CCTV camera – was one of numerous novelties laid on for guests, along with a farm shop and Thai massages. Not to mention a restaurant with a ceiling made of wine bottles, which made you feel as if you were dining on a hidden floor beneath an oenophile's cellar.

The party on 21 June 2014 marked the end of a gruelling few months setting up the business and gaining the necessary regulatory approvals needed to launch. Woodford's staff and a group of project managers who had helped get the business up and running mingled and drank beer and champagne in the eclectic gardens.

It was also the celebration of a new start. Passing by a life-sized carved lion, there was Craig Newman – a man who former colleagues had often compared to the same creature but who now seemed very far from roaring in displeasure. As for Neil Woodford, the hero of the hour, memories of his shouting at the wall to let off steam on his Invesco Perpetual lunchbreaks were long forgotten. Amid the palm fronds and champagne, instead of yelling at plasterwork, the man of the hour was about to address his people.

They wondered what he would say. With the business technicalities in place and the hype building, the world seemed his for the taking. Perhaps he'd emphasise the benefits of the new-found freedom they would all have at his budding investment empire; outline his vision for a style of fund management that put the interests of its investors first; reiterate his desire to lead the way in corporate governance?

It was still relatively early in the evening when the man of the hour stepped out to say his piece. He struck a bulkier figure than ever, a corporate prop forward of a man, his thinning hair now buzzed incredibly short and turning a faint grey in the summer twilight.

But the words didn't come. Or, not many of them. What he had to say was so brief and quiet that few who attended could later remember it at all.

Then again, after the £20 glasses of champagne came the shots…

———————

In the professional world, as the pundits had predicted, Woodford breezed through the launch of his new business. He had no problem at all attracting investors. "The launch could not have gone better. We were the talk of the town and everybody loved us," says one of Woodford's former colleagues.

The amount of money that flooded into the business during the first few weeks was astonishing. Between 2 June and 19 June – the so-called 'offer period', when investors were enticed into the fund before it began trading – it raised £1.6bn. It was the largest amount ever gathered for the launch of a UK open-ended fund, a common structure for investments used by Woodford which offers investors daily liquidity. (Having daily liquidity allows savers to easily access their cash, rather than other types of investment fund which require their money to be tied up for longer periods.)

It wasn't just ordinary savers who were putting their money with Woodford. Large City investors also piled into the Equity

Income fund, with around £900m coming from Jupiter, the UK asset manager which had invested with Woodford during his time at Invesco. One of the biggest backers was UK wealth management firm St James's Place, which handed Woodford a lucrative £3.7bn mandate to manage on their behalf. Aviva Investors also signed over a chunk of cash to be managed for its pension customers. Kent County Council, one of Woodford's most loyal clients from his time at Invesco Perpetual having invested with him since 2007, also committed £200m to his new fund.

A significant proportion of the new money originated from retail customers using Hargreaves Lansdown, a popular investment platform which heavily promoted Woodford's fund in the run-up to its launch.

Just weeks after opening the doors to his new operation, Woodford had gathered £5bn from investors. It was an incredible vote of confidence and an unbelievable start for a new business. Some of Woodford's colleagues were rewarded with large windfalls as a result. At least two members of the sales team received £300,000 bonuses in the early stage of the business being established, according to one former employee. This was despite the bulk of the money originating from Woodford's old contacts.

Several months after the launch, Woodford also treated himself − buying a new Ferrari which he track tested in Maranello, Italy, along with his business partner Newman. Newman and Woodford's obsession with fast cars was not lost on other members of staff. The car park often resembled a high-end car showroom forecourt. "Every lunchtime we'd go out and look at what cars had turned up. They were very flashy," says one former employee. "Craig had good taste in cars. You could definitely hear he had arrived when he drove into the car park." Woodford's gamble to leave Invesco Perpetual appeared to have paid off.

Woodford was lauded for something unusual he did a month after launching Equity Income: he disclosed a full list of his holdings. Typically fund managers only reveal their fund's top ten positions. Woodford sought to win over investors and the powerful consumer press with the message that investors should know exactly where their money was being put to work. It was admirable – even if Woodford's transparent approach to his portfolio holdings would later accelerate his downfall when his largest fund ran into trouble.

"It was a revolutionary move for a retail fund to be highly transparent, and not the standard process for most fund management companies," says Jason Hollands, a managing director at online investment platform Bestinvest. "Most fund managers are reluctant to disclose their positions. They would argue it gives away their USP. I suspect, because of what happened to Woodford, few others will want to go down that route."

The portfolio breakdown showed Woodford's largest holding in his new fund was pharmaceutical giant AstraZeneca, with just over 8% of assets invested in the drugmaker. Just months before launching his new business, Woodford had been among vocal investors who opposed a £69bn takeover bid by US rival

Pfizer, claiming he could make more money for investors if AstraZeneca remained independent.

Some of Woodford's largest stakes were in companies that had helped him deliver consistent returns for his investors while at Invesco, including British American Tobacco, Imperial Tobacco and Reynolds American. Woodford's desire to invest in early-stage companies was evident, with a significant chunk of his new fund devoted to Imperial Innovations. This technology-focused investment firm invested in life science and technology companies, with links to universities including Imperial College London, Oxford and Cambridge. It was listed on the Alternative Investment Market (AIM), a division of the London Stock Exchange where smaller companies list to raise capital from shareholders.

In fact, there were several AIM-listed stocks within Woodford's Equity Income fund, including biotech company e-Therapeutics, life sciences focused Retroscreen Virology and 4D Pharma, which focused on live biotherapeutic products. Other fledgling companies to receive Woodford's backing were immunotherapy developer Circassia, vaccine company Retroscreen Virology and community broadband business Gigaclear.

To some, the portfolio signalled a distinct shift in Woodford's investment style. This would later be heavily scrutinised for the role it played in bringing down his flagship fund. "The big issue was the nature of the positions," says a former colleague of Woodford's. "You would not expect a fund with 'income' in the name to have such a large percentage in biotech and healthcare stocks, most of which have no yield whatsoever. Investors stuck by him in the belief that he had been through tough periods before and would bounce back. But they didn't appreciate what they were invested in was different from the Woodford of old."

HSBC was the only bank that made it into Woodford's new fund – little surprise given his aversion to lenders during his time in Henley, which had allowed him to sail through the financial crisis unscathed. Woodford had started to build a position in HSBC a year previously via the investment mandate he ran for St James's Place, making it the first time he had invested in a bank since 2002. However, this investment was only a fleeting one. Just three months after including HSBC in his Equity Income fund, Woodford announced that he was dumping this holding completely, citing concerns over the bank's ability to pay any looming financial penalties.

Woodford wanted to create a distinct culture at his new business, not unlike some of the technology firms into which he had started to plough millions of pounds. Described by one former colleague as a "two-fingered typist", Woodford may not have been the most adept with technology, but he wanted the business to be a digital-first operation. Everything from trading to ordering sandwiches for client meetings was done via a digital interface. The office operated a paperless policy, with documents shared and viewed on laptops and iPads. Staff were encouraged to communicate with each other via Slack, the online corporate messaging system. When working from home, it was not uncommon to find

Woodford logged on the company's Slack channel at 11pm on a Saturday night.

Woodford worked from home at least once a week, phoning in or emailing dealing instructions to the trading desk who would then input this information to execute a trade. Woodford's IT team was developing an app that would make this process more efficient and possible without the need of a Bloomberg terminal, but it only ever reached the development stage.

The office had a distinct start-up vibe. There was a barista-run coffee lounge, no limits on staff holidays and a relaxed dress policy. Newman led by example on this, often wearing hoodies and plaid shirts to work, while Woodford was comfortable in jeans, sweatshirt and trainers. The firm tried its best to eschew the stuffy image of fund management.

While some staff received large bonus payments after the business was set up, Woodford and Newman introduced an unusual policy in 2016: scrapping bonus payments for its entire 35-strong workforce. They claimed bonuses were not in keeping with the long-term approach the company wanted to take regarding investments, and that bonus payments rarely improved performance. Staff were given a pay rise that year to avoid being out of pocket – but told their salaries would remain fixed in future.

It was another way Woodford sought to differentiate himself from his fund management rivals, some of which paid out millions of pounds in bonuses each year, often when they had failed to deliver strong performance. "No other firm had taken a stringent line on variable pay and it was genuinely ground-breaking at the time," says Tim Wright, a remuneration specialist who works with asset management firms. "Some in the industry thought it was a brave move, others thought it was mad. What was noticeable was that nobody at the time said they would follow suit."

To those watching from a distance, things could not be going better for Woodford. But trouble was already starting to brew within the company.

II

It began when Smith and Hamilton, two of the original partners, announced they were quitting just six months after helping Woodford set up the business. The departures were unexpected. Those working at Woodford's new organisation sensed tensions among the partners reached boiling point after Hamilton and Smith began to challenge some of the investments Woodford was making in relatively unknown companies.

"The whole point of leaving Invesco was not to be hemmed in by compliance," says one former colleague. "But Neil believed his skills were transferable to private companies. They weren't."

The departure of the two sceptics – half the founding partners – did not, however, give Woodford pause for thought. Instead, he intensified his pursuit of small and obscure companies. Woodford and Newman turned their attention to another new fund. April 2015 saw the launch of Patient Capital, a listed investment trust which aimed to invest in smaller companies offering attractive growth opportunities. Listed on the stock market, investment trusts have different characteristics to open-ended funds. Most notably, they have a fixed pool of capital and savers invest by purchasing shares in the trust on the stock market. They also have a board of directors, which is meant to provide an additional layer of oversight and bolster investor protection. Unlike Woodford's flagship Equity Income fund – which included large, well-established companies – the trust would expose investors to between 60 and 80 lesser-known businesses, including companies not yet listed on the stock market.

Woodford outlined his ambition to make significant investments in start-up companies in an article he penned for *Investors Chronicle* towards the end of 2014. "Early-stage businesses are an unloved, undervalued asset class that I believe offers huge untapped potential," he wrote. Woodford acknowledged that the risks of investing in such companies was "higher than in the more mainstream investment universe", but argued that despite this the potential rewards on offer "look extremely attractive".

"Although these early-stage investments may be small in a portfolio context initially, we expect them to become bigger as they mature," he wrote. "In many respects my team and I view all other stocks in the portfolio in the same way. We look at all companies through the same valuation lens, whether they are FTSE 100, midcap, AIM-listed or unquoted."[36]

For some, adopting this approach did not make sense. "How

can you value stocks that are pre-profitable?" says Hollands from Bestinvest. "Venture capital is a very different investment process to being invested in big liquid stocks with lots of free cash flow. A typical venture capital outfit is very research-intensive, with 15 investment professionals."

Nevertheless, Woodford's thinking struck a chord with investors. Patient Capital pulled in £800m at its launch – another record fundraising, this time for a listed investment trust. (The previous record had been set more than 20 years earlier, when the Mercury European Privatisation Investment trust garnered £540m.)[37]

With his second fund up and running, Woodford's empire had now amassed more than £9bn from investors, with the majority sitting in his flagship Equity Income product. But there was one more opportunity to pull in investors. In March 2017, Woodford launched his Income Focus fund, promising access to a more concentrated number of companies with the potential to generate higher returns than his main Equity Income fund. It proved another smart move, raising more than £550m. The Income Focus fund started off with 50 holdings, compared to 131 in the Equity Income.[38]

By the middle of 2017, assets in the Equity Income fund had ballooned to £10.2bn, and it had returned close to 40% since its launch, comfortably beating the 25.7% performance posted by the average fund in the same sector. Woodford appeared to be on an unstoppable trajectory. His company was also doing extremely well financially, posting a £35.4m profit in the year to March 2016. Woodford and Newman pocketed £7.2m and £3.9m respectively that year.

———————

The sharp rise in assets coincided with another expensive purchase for Woodford – a six-bedroom holiday home in Salcombe, Devon. Woodford and his wife bought the property for more than £6m in 2017 and spent considerable amounts of money extending and fitting it out with slate floors, a gym and wooden balconies. The *Daily Mail* likened the house, perched halfway up a cliff, to a "Bond villain's lair".[39]

By now, the company was in full swing. Woodford's operation grew to around 40 staff, although only a handful were women, including the head of HR and Woodford and Newman's personal assistants. An army of contractors was drafted in to help with various IT projects; at times they outnumbered permanent members of staff.

Despite the move away from Henley, some of Woodford's work habits remained the same. He kept a glass-partitioned office away from the rest of the staff in order to absorb himself in managing the billions of pounds he had amassed from clients. It also made it easy to sense when Woodford's anger was beginning to bubble over. "You could definitely hear Neil having a little moment in his office," says one former colleague. "Because it was glass you could hear everything. It would never be *at* someone – it would always be frustration at whatever work he was doing at the time."

Woodford had established an impressive empire in an incredibly short amount of time. But those working closest to him sensed he had a personal ambition to prove himself to his former employer. "We talked about building a transformational business, but the under-current was always 'we need to get all the money from Invesco'. I don't think Neil and Craig would have been happy until every last penny had been switched over," says another ex-colleague.

5

Since I've Been Loving You

The loudest cheerleader

I

NEIL WOODFORD rarely had a good reason to wear a tie, but this was a special occasion and he needed to look the part. It was just days before the official launch of his Equity Income fund. Woodford was getting ready to be interviewed for a promotional video that would be aired on the website of Hargreaves Lansdown, now the UK's biggest investment platform. The Bristol-based company had pulled out all the stops, kitting out a studio and drafting in a freelance journalist to quiz Woodford about his new fund and the reasons why investors should put money into his new venture.

The slick footage could easily have passed as a job interview. Woodford was asked why he decided to strike out on his own and to explain his forecast for the UK economy over the next five years. He sat back in an uncomfortable-looking office chair, his hands clasped together, and sought to reassure any doubters. He told viewers that his approach to managing investors' money would be very similar to the one he followed at Invesco Perpetual. He stressed it would be "business as usual", only this time he would be free from any bureaucracy that came with working within a large organisation – and could focus purely on managing money.

But this was Woodford's chance to tout his new fund to tens of thousands of potential investors, and he was also keen to explain how he had an edge over his competitors. "The crucial difference is that my long-term investment perspective helps me make better judgements," he said.

———

Woodford was idolised not only by the thousands of investors he had made a small fortune for during his tenure at Invesco Perpetual, but also by the firm through which many increasingly invested with him: Hargreaves Lansdown. It was, perhaps, little wonder – the company made tens of millions of pounds in fees by promoting his funds to the British public.

Founded in a spare bedroom in 1981 by two friends, Peter Hargreaves and Stephen Lansdown, the company began its existence offering unit trusts to investors via newspaper adverts, as well as assistance with tax planning. It went on to amass an army of almost 1.5 million customers and close to 1,600 staff.

Its listing on the stock market in May 2007 made its two founders multi-millionaires overnight, and both have seen their wealth multiply several times over since then. Lancashire-born Hargreaves is worth an estimated £2.4bn, according to the *Sunday Times* Rich List, ranking him as the 58th wealthiest person in the UK.[40] Lansdown, the largest shareholder in Bristol City Football Club, has accumulated a smaller, but still impressive, £1.4bn personal fortune.

The ruddy-faced Hargreaves is arguably one of the most frugal billionaires in the world. He has refused to move abroad to save on his personal tax bill or spend his money on the trappings of wealth, such as fast cars or yachts.[41] He is a keen political donor, having given more than £3m to the campaign to leave the European Union in 2016 and writing a £1m cheque to the Conservative Party ahead of the general election in 2019. Hargreaves was chief executive of the business until 2010 but remained on the board as an executive director until 2015 and is still one of the company's major shareholders.

The investment platform has huge sway in the UK investment market, offering access to more than 3,000 different types of investments and overseeing more than £100bn of customer savings. Soon after Woodford announced his intention to launch a new business and fund, Hargreaves Lansdown's marketing machine went into overdrive, with full-page advertisements taken out in the financial press, as well as postal promotions and digital advertising targeting its clients. "Woodford was revered as much as a superstar internally as he was externally", says one former Hargreaves Lansdown employee.

Hargreaves Lansdown prides itself on the research it dedicates to investment funds, but it also has an immensely powerful marketing arm. "They can really get a lot done in a short space of time and be willing to put millions of pounds behind press advertising, mail shots and email campaigns," says the former employee. "That was certainly what happened with Woodford."

Hargreaves Lansdown had past experience with other big marketing drives designed to drum up maximum interest among retail investors, such as the much-anticipated stock market listing of Royal Mail in 2013. Its advertising push in the run-up to this listing – which was heavily oversubscribed as investors frantically tried to snap up shares – won Hargreaves Lansdown almost 30,000 new clients and increased assets on its platform by £13bn that year.

While the Royal Mail flotation had helped Hargreaves Lansdown secure a large number of retail investors looking to trade shares, the rewards for promoting Woodford were far more attractive. The funds business was the largest revenue generator for Hargreaves. Now it had the UK's best-performing stock-picker on board.

The promotional material sent out to Hargreaves Lansdown clients ahead of Woodford's first fund launch could not have been more effusive. Its billionaire founder was glowing about the fund manager's potential. "We believe his skills are undoubted and his wealth of experience means that he has the courage to back his convictions," Hargreaves told investors in promotional literature backing the fund. "I will be investing at launch and I suggest investors consider doing the same."

Mark Dampier, Hargreaves Lansdown's head of research who had known Woodford for more than two decades, was equally glowing. He described him as "one of the finest fund managers of his generation" and told platform customers that he and his wife would both be investing in the fund at launch.

Dampier was a hugely influential figure within the FTSE 100 broker and accumulated millions of pounds worth of shares in Hargreaves Lansdown, where he worked from 1998 until his retirement in August 2020. He was also the architect of the influential Wealth 150 list, a selection of the platform's most favoured funds, which would later attract intense media scrutiny for its decision to include Woodford's fund even as the wheels began to fall off.

II

On the second floor of Hargreaves Lansdown's Bristol office sits a cohort of the investment company's most powerful executives.

It is where Dampier sat with his team, close to colleagues who oversaw the company's multi-manager funds, led by Lee Gardhouse. Some of Hargreaves Lansdown's most recognisable spokespeople – including Tom McPhail, Danny Cox and Laith Khalaf – also had desks dotted around this influential corner of the office.

Despite stepping down as CEO – and, in his autobiography, insisting that meetings should always be held without chairs in order to boost efficiency[42] – Hargreaves had a seat next to the research team, while Ian Gorham, who was CEO until 2017, sat just a few feet away.

"Peter would never have weighed in on research discussions, but there was always a different feel when he was in the office. There were some strong personalities around," says a former Hargreaves Lansdown employee.

In the run-up to Woodford's debut fund launch, this part of the office became a hive of activity, as colleagues from the marketing team hurried back and forth to the research desk to discuss content ideas to include in upcoming promotion material. The silver-haired Dampier was instantly recognisable to Hargreaves Lansdown investors. His lightly bearded face – always set in a cheerful grin – frequently appeared next to articles he wrote for the platform's *Investment Times* magazine, and he conducted video interviews with Woodford discussing the outlook for his funds.

Woodford's stature earned his new fund automatic entry onto Hargreaves Lansdown's prized Wealth 150 list. Dampier was ultimately responsible for the list, created in 2003, which was reserved for funds which passed a rigorous research process. Woodford's new fund had no track record. But Dampier said he had "no hesitation" in admitting it to the platform's hall of fame given the stellar performance he had achieved at Invesco Perpetual.

Later, in 2015, Dampier published a book called *Effective*

Investing. Here he described Woodford's Equity Income as one of his top ten holdings in his own self-invested personal pension. In the same book, he wrote that "[t]he biggest investment in my ISA – around 40% – is made up of the shares I own in Hargreaves Lansdown. Next is the Woodford Patient Capital Trust". Of the latter he said: "I am hoping for some great long-term capital gains from this".[43]

Wealth 150 was just one of several so-called buy lists offered by investment platforms in the UK, which help clients select funds by narrowing down thousands of options. They have become increasingly popular as more savers take investment matters into their own hands, often investing online rather than seek out financial advice.

Some began to question the amount of scrutiny that Woodford's new fund received before being included on the Wealth 150 list. "Given the scale of the fund launch and the excitement surrounding it, which Hargreaves contributed to, I thought there would have been more belt and braces analysis," says one ex-Hargreaves Lansdown staffer. "It felt more like this is the best marketing opportunity we would ever come across and that Neil and his investment skill had already been addressed while he was at Invesco, so we weren't going to challenge it again."

On the rare occasions Woodford visited the Bristol office, presentations from the fund manager were light on detail. "There was no real challenge or interrogation about his process," says the former Hargreaves Lansdown employee. "It would just be an update on his fund. Given how many hundreds of millions were invested in his fund on clients' behalf, you need more than that."

Hargreaves Lansdown had thrown considerable weight behind Woodford's new fund and had negotiated a discounted fee for their clients, meaning they would pay 0.6% for Equity Income rather than 0.75% elsewhere. When its Wealth 150 was relaunched and rebranded as the Wealth 50 in January 2019, the fee was brought down further to 0.5% a year.

At that point, Woodford was six months away from disaster.

———————

Hargreaves Lansdown boasts that it has the necessary bargaining power to bring down costs and charges for its clients. The platform claimed to have saved its customers more than £61m in fees during 2018 alone due to the lower charges it negotiated with some fund managers.[44] But buy lists, which are not regulated, have been criticised for being nothing more than a marketing gimmick – with some claiming certain funds are given pride of place because of their potential to generate more business for platforms, particularly blockbuster products where there is high investor demand.

Lists of recommended funds are hugely influential. Obtaining independent financial advice has become more expensive in the UK following regulatory changes which ban advisers from receiving commission payments for recommending certain products. As a result, a growing number of retail investors have taken personal finance decisions into their own hands and have come to rely more on these lists when it comes to choosing investments.

For fund managers, being included on a list of recommended products can bring huge advantages. A study by the FCA in 2017 found that for every year following the addition of a fund to a platform's buy list and while it was still recommended, a fund will gather average inflows of £5.9m.[45] In the case of Hargreaves Lansdown, Woodford had agreed a fee discount making investment via the platform the cheapest way to access his Equity Income fund. On top of Woodford's fee, Hargreaves Lansdown levied a 0.45% charge, calculated on the amount they had in Woodford's fund.

The more money Hargreaves Lansdown could attract to Woodford's blockbuster fund, the more the platform stood to reap in revenues.

Terry Smith, one of the best-selling fund managers in the UK, has been a persistent critic of Hargreaves Lansdown for failing to include his best-selling Fundsmith Equity fund on its recommended buy list, despite an impressive performance track record. Smith's fund has returned more than 400% since its launch and now manages over £20bn in assets – double what Woodford's Equity Income fund oversaw at its peak in 2017. Smith claims Hargreaves Lansdown has consistently refused to include his fund on its buy list because his charging structure is at odds with their fee model.

"Every conversation we have ever had with Hargreaves Lansdown has really been about our unwillingness to cut them a special deal," he says. Smith claims exclusive fees negotiated between fund managers and platforms can be problematic for investors, who may wish in future to move their assets to another platform provider which does not have the same fee agreement.

"Let's imagine you were invested in the Woodford fund on the Hargreaves Lansdown platform with the special fee discount. You might be happy with Woodford but you might not be happy with Hargreaves, so you want to go elsewhere. This would technically be a redemption as another platform would not have the same share class, so you get handed a capital gains tax bill. That's just one unintended consequence."

A decade on from the launch of his equity fund, Smith has made his peace with the fact that he may never make it onto the Hargreaves Lansdown list, having criticised the research process which drives it. "I don't care if I'm not on their buy list. In fact, I'd be worried if I *was* on it," he says.

Most recently Hargreaves Lansdown said Smith's refusal to provide monthly holdings and liquidity data prevented Fundsmith Equity from making the cut.

Emma Wall, head of investment analysis at Hargreaves Lansdown, says: "We need this data in order to do full qualitative and quantitative analysis of the fund and the manager's track record, determine how we might expect the fund to perform in the future, and keep up to date with portfolio changes. Some fund managers do not provide this data on a regular enough basis, and therefore we are unable to do the necessary analysis, including Fundsmith who prefer to provide data on a six-month basis rather than monthly.

"Analysis of the latest data we have suggests that it is likely

Fundsmith would make the list, but we can't make exceptions to our enhanced commitment to governance and risk management."

The relationship with Woodford would prove extremely lucrative for Hargreaves Lansdown. Over the four years Woodford's Equity Income was promoted on the platform's preferred list of funds, Hargreaves Lansdown raked in fees of more than £40m, around 2% of all revenue the entire business generated over the same period.

Almost 134,000 Hargreaves Lansdown customers had directly invested in Woodford's biggest fund. The average amount held by each investor was just over £8,000. But there were more than 150,000 other Hargreaves Lansdown customers exposed to Woodford. As well as customers who had chosen to invest in Woodford directly, others were invested in his flagship fund via the platform's own multi-manager funds.

These are a suite of ten funds overseen by Hargreaves Lansdown's own fund managers, which invest in other funds such as those run by Woodford. Six of these multi-manager funds were also invested in Woodford's flagship Equity Income product. Overall, Hargreaves Lansdown customers had £1.6bn invested in Woodford's fund by June 2019.

Hargreaves Lansdown's multi-manager team, led by Lee Gardhouse, became an increasingly important revenue generator for the business after the regulatory changes in 2013 which banned commission payments for recommending certain products. "Don't underestimate the importance of Hargreaves' own multi-manager funds," says another former

Hargreaves Lansdown employee. "The company had to switch from selling other people's funds to selling its own internal stuff. At that point Lee and his team became much more important within the business."

Some began to question the relationship with Woodford and why he had been put on the Wealth 150 list by default. The concern was that more attention seemed to have been paid to the individual fund manager rather than the contents of the actual fund he was running and its suitability for Hargreaves Lansdown clients.

Even as performance of Woodford's main fund began to wane, Hargreaves Lansdown stuck by the fund manager. His product remained on its influential buy list. "We believe it's premature to write Neil Woodford off," an article penned by Hargreaves Lansdown's head of investment analysis Richard Troue said in January 2018.[46] By that point, investors had already started to flee Equity Income on the back of performance concerns, with assets in the fund falling by £1.5bn in 2017.

"When a fund manager underperforms, investors are naturally keen to understand why, so they can make a decision whether to stick with the fund," Troue went on to say. "When the fund in question is managed by Neil Woodford, one of the highest-profile fund managers in the UK, the negative press it generates can be blown out of proportion."

The outflows were enough to prompt another video interview with Hargreaves Lansdown, although this time Woodford had ditched the suit and tie and appeared in his trademark black sweater and jeans. The location was

Woodford's Oxford headquarters. Colourful artwork dotted the white walls. Dampier sat across from the fund manager in a stylish lounge chair. The mood was distinctly different from the video staged just before Woodford's fund launch. Rather than trying to sell his fund, this was an opportunity for Woodford to "put things in perspective", according to Hargreaves Lansdown's website.

As questions began to mount over Woodford's exposure to unquoted companies, which had risen to around 9.5% by this point, Dampier asked if Woodford felt the fund had become more risky as a result. "No, I don't," Woodford said. "Clearly these are younger businesses, people perceive them to be much riskier than a more mature business, and to some extent I wouldn't pick a fight with people who argue that. But I think the perception of risk is way out of kilter with the reality." Woodford's defence was that many of the younger companies he was invested in had already passed the riskier stage of their development, moving from early-stage ideas through to commercialisation.

Even as performance of Woodford's Equity Income fund began to be called into question by financial pundits and the media, it remained featured on Hargreaves Lansdown's influential buy list. Questions began to be asked about the relationship between the UK's largest investment platform and the country's best-selling fund manager, and whether enough was being done to keep Woodford in check. Having backed Woodford heavily from the start, airing concerns about his performance or stock-picking approach would not only potentially scare off investors, it would also cause major embarrassment

"Hargreaves Lansdown knew they had spent so much time and money promoting this guy, realistically what could they do?" says a former Hargreaves Lansdown employee. "They'd look like fools if they turned around in three years and said Neil had gone off the rails."

The close connection between Woodford and Hargreaves Lansdown would come under intense scrutiny in the months following the suspension of his largest fund. In the month leading up to Woodford's fund being frozen, Dampier and his wife Annette, along with Gardhouse, sold shares in Hargreaves Lansdown worth more than £6m. The timing might have been coincidental and simply a way to cash profits on the back of Hargreaves Lansdown's rising share price, which reached a historic high during May 2019. Dampier still had money tied up in Equity Income when it was suspended, as well as Woodford's other two funds, and never sold any of his Woodford holdings. But their actions helped them avoid a period where the Woodford fallout sparked a double-digit drop in the stock price as the company became embroiled in the controversy.

Meanwhile Chris Hill, CEO of Hargreaves Lansdown, was doing his best to placate angry Woodford investors who wanted answers about why a fund that was now frozen had been promoted for so long. Hill offered an apology to the thousands of customers whose savings were now locked in with Woodford, telling them he shared their "disappointment and frustration". He later announced that he would forego his bonus – £1.7m in 2017 – with Dampier and Gardhouse adopting the same approach.

Hargreaves Lansdown now had to do some soul searching about the support it had given Woodford, in particular allowing his fund to be included on its buy list – and to remain there right up to the moment of its suspension. Its loyalty to Woodford had angered one man in particular. Peter Hargreaves, co-founder of the firm, had not been able to contain his displeasure any longer.

"It's annoyed the hell out of me that it would appear he [Woodford] has not been truthful with Hargreaves Lansdown. But it's also annoyed me that they let it go on so long," Hargreaves told the *Sunday Times* a month before Woodford's empire eventually collapsed. "Woodford has been in this situation before and had always come good and the last thing you want to do is tell your investors to sell and next week it all goes right. The problem was Hargreaves Lansdown had too much with him."[47]

Ironically, in 2015, the man who had endorsed Woodford's new funds so readily had come close to putting his finger on the problems that would later emerge, when he defended fund managers who hit rough patches. In his book, Dampier wrote: "If the market falls and a fund manager like Anthony Bolton, Neil Woodford or Nigel Thomas does poorly, it does not mean that they have become bad fund managers overnight. In fact, they're the ones who thanks to experience will keep their nerve, which is what you need. What you don't want is someone suddenly going off-base because something's happened to the market and *he's doing something he wouldn't normally do. That's normally a recipe for disaster."*[48] [Emphasis added.]

In this case, Woodford hadn't been doing poorly in response to an overall market fall – but he certainly had begun doing things he wouldn't normally do.

6

You Shook Me

The liquidity trap

I

ANDREA ROSSI, an eccentric Italian entrepreneur and inventor, was standing in the doorway of his makeshift laboratory in Bologna getting ready to demonstrate his groundbreaking invention.

The set-up resembled a kitchen crossed with a garage workshop. Disorder reigned. An amp meter was plugged into a mains wall socket. A water pump and four small cylinders were perched on a table, connected to a spiralling network of tubes. Large hydrogen canisters were dotted around the room, while a black hose was fed through a hole in the wall leading to a sink. The chaotic scene in Bologna was a world away from the plush corporate boardrooms of the blue-chip stocks in which

Woodford had traditionally invested. But Rossi's device would later be a key factor in one of the biggest and most controversial investments made by Woodford.

Steven Krivit, an investigative science journalist and expert on low-energy nuclear reaction research, was filming Rossi. The inventor had claimed to have designed a commercially viable way of generating energy using the same nuclear reaction which powers the sun, but at room temperature – otherwise known as cold fusion.

It was a potential breakthrough which scientists have been trying to achieve for decades. All Rossi had to do was prove that it worked.[49]

"Welcome to my laboratory", Rossi said in a thick Italian accent. Dressed in a light blue shirt and tie, Rossi proceeded to pace the tiled floor with a small pocket calculator in one hand, using the other to point to various gauges and thermometers. He paused at various pieces of equipment and put on his reading glasses as he checked the measurements.

For all the equipment laid out in the room, the end result was something of an anti-climax. To the layman, all Rossi's device had produced was a few puffs of steam coming from the end of a hose. Not long after Krivit uploaded his video of Rossi on his website, scientists and engineers began to pick holes in his device and question whether the inventor was nothing more than an elaborate con artist. Krivit says he harboured his own doubts about Rossi for around a year before he filmed him in Italy. Rossi's behaviour in the weeks leading up to their meeting aroused yet more suspicion.

"I asked Rossi background questions and softball questions. He was very friendly, appeared confident, and welcoming in response to my request. This softened my previous hard judgment of him and his claims," says Krivit. "But about two weeks before the interview date I began to ask Rossi for documents that showed actual data. That's when he began to deflect and not respond to my questions."

Rossi had a chequered past. During the 1970s, he founded a company called Petroldragon, having claimed to have discovered a way to convert large-scale industrial waste, such as old tyres, into fuel. However, the operation was forced to close and led to Rossi being arrested for environmental crimes and tax fraud, although he was later acquitted of most charges.[50]

Yet, despite Rossi's past and the cold fusion community trying to debunk his so-called E Cat invention, he managed to attract the attention of Tom Darden, the chief executive of Cherokee Investment Partners, a private equity firm located in North Carolina. Darden agreed to licence Rossi's technology and established Industrial Heat in 2012 to attract investment in an attempt to commercialise the invention. Hollywood actor Brad Pitt and Steve Jobs' widow Laurene Powell Jobs were among the most famous names who threw their financial backing behind the firm.[51]

Neil Woodford also invested more than £50m of his investors' money in Industrial Heat via both his Equity Income fund and Patient Capital trust.

Rossi was paid $11.5m by Industrial Heat after conducting his own due diligence tests on the technology, but the relationship between the two parties soured in 2016, ending in a lawsuit in which Rossi claimed he was owed $89m as part of the licensing agreement. In an email to Woodford and his team on 3 March 2016, Industrial Heat's chief operating officer JT Vaughan delivered the news that it had not been able to independently test Rossi's technology. It was a blow for Woodford: Industrial Heat was one of the largest holdings in his Patient Capital trust.

Paul Lamacraft, one of Woodford's fund managers, responded by email to Vaughan, saying: "This is clearly very disappointing given that Rossi's technology was a core element of the initial investment."[52] Rossi and Industrial Heat settled out of court and the two parties went their separate ways. But Woodford's punt on Industrial Heat was just one example of how he had begun to plough money into companies way beyond the realm of the large-cap listed stocks that had made him and his investors a fortune during his career.

———————

One former colleague of Woodford's says there was a lack of due diligence performed on some of the early-stage companies that began knocking on their door seeking investment. "Successful private equity people or venture capitalists will tell you they have a process to weed out people," says the former colleague. "The pitches might be polished, but you have to pick it apart and kick the wheels. Documents were very much taken at face value."

The brakes were applied to at least one potential multi-million-pound investment after alarm bells were sounded when the company seeking capital bombarded Woodford's team for progress updates, according to one former employee. At one point, representatives from the company telephoned one of Woodford's team from the Shell petrol station across the road from the Garsington Road office, offering to provide further documents that might be needed to quickly confirm the investment. The odd behaviour immediately aroused suspicion.

The experience with Industrial Heat had brought home to Woodford's team the high stakes involved when investing in smaller companies. But their exposure to unlisted companies was high, making up 65% of the assets in Patient Capital trust by the end of 2018. Ordinarily this would not have been a problem, but trouble was on the horizon for Woodford. He was starting to experience an increase in requests from investors wanting their money back from his main Equity Income fund, which also held some of the same unquoted positions.

Some of the investments Woodford was making in relatively unknown companies would later prove a major headache for him as he sought to raise enough money to pay back those investors wanting to jump ship. Benevolent AI, which uses artificial intelligence to search for new drug treatments, was the largest unquoted holding in Patient Capital, but also a top position in Woodford's flagship fund. Woodford was an early backer of the London-based start-up and the company's valuation at one point topped $2bn. Verseon, another biotech start-up which had a blockbuster listing on the alternative investment market in 2015, was also a Woodford favourite and included among the Equity Income fund's holdings.

But the fund manager's appetite to back companies of this nature was starting to attract the wrong kind of attention, particularly from other professional investors who could sense he was straying into areas he knew nothing about. "Woodford had two successful calls: avoiding dotcom and the financial crash. There is a world of difference between that and being an investor in biotechnology stocks. What on earth would lead you to think you had an ability in that?" says one fund manager.

Woodford's holdings in some of these early-stage companies would later prove highly problematic, but he wasn't willing to sell what he perceived to be good investments. He believed some would eventually list on some of the world's biggest stock markets, which in turn would bring down his exposure to unquoted companies as these companies became listed entities. In the meantime, Woodford had to come up with a way of ensuring he could continue to back some of his favourite picks but still play by the rules of the game.

II

Towards the end of 2017 Woodford was skirting dangerously close to the limits he was meant to adhere to concerning his investments in unquoted companies. Open-ended investment funds like Woodford's Equity Income have to abide by a key European Union regulatory framework, known as Ucits, which places a 10% threshold on the amount of assets that can be invested in unquoted companies.

Ucits is regarded as one of Europe's biggest success stories – at least among those in the investment world – and investors as far away as Asia choose to invest in EU funds they know are under the close watch of regulators. Funds under this regime also allow investors to get their money back at short notice, rather than some investments which tie in customers for much longer periods of time. The 10% cap on unquoted assets is to ensure funds have enough investments in companies that are highly liquid, meaning their shares are easier to sell in the event that a large number of investors want to pull their money en masse.

Woodford had already started to stray into unquoted companies during his time at Invesco Perpetual, but there his allocations had not been large enough to cause concern. "It wasn't as though he was going wildly into the woods," says Darius McDermott from Chelsea Financial Services. "It was never more than 5% of his Income and High Income funds [at Invesco Perpetual]. Neil's view on banks, oil or tobacco was always more important to the returns he generated than whether he had a small holding in an unlisted company. It was never really a big part of what he did."

Now, Woodford's increasing urge to invest more money into lesser-known companies began to put a strain on the relationship with Hargreaves Lansdown. The investment platform had begun to privately express concerns about Woodford's approach in November 2017, when it noticed a rise in the proportion of small and unlisted assets in the Equity Income fund. Dampier met with Woodford that same month and sought reassurance that the issue would be addressed. Woodford and his team told Hargreaves Lansdown no new investments would be made into unquoted businesses.

There was nothing unusual in the meetings themselves. Woodford and Hargreaves Lansdown had met on more than 30 occasions since the platform included his Equity Income fund on its buy list. But there was a sense that Woodford was not being entirely frank with his friends in Bristol. Concerns were starting to be raised internally within Hargreaves Lansdown about Woodford's approach, and not just about the one taken by his main equity fund.

"With Income Focus, the idea was this was just to be the income players. But there was a feeling that it was sold as an income fund and was actually investing in high-risk, illiquid holdings," says a former Hargreaves Lansdown employee. Hargreaves Lansdown requested that Woodford and his team stick closely to the strict EU rules on investing in unquoted companies and reduce early-warning thresholds to ensure they didn't breach the limit. It was a red line they were not willing to let him cross. Woodford promised to immediately inform the platform if the limit was breached.

Woodford's fund went on to exceed the 10% limit twice several months later – once in February 2018 and again in March. But he did not tell Hargreaves Lansdown. Woodford and his team later claimed the agreement to notify Hargreaves Lansdown covered month-end breaches only, not those occurring inadvertently during the month.

Woodford had to come up with a way of keeping hold of some of what he thought were the most promising unquoted companies, while also ensuring his fund did not breach regulatory limits. One unconventional manouevre he instigated was to transfer £73m worth of unquoted stocks from one fund to another. The decision would see the Equity Income fund sell stakes in five unquoted firms to the Patient Capital trust in exchange for shares. It helped bring down the percentage that Woodford's flagship fund held in unquoted companies.

Another unusual move was to list some of his unquoted holdings on the International Stock Exchange (TISE) in Guernsey, a tiny bourse which counts Hargreaves Lansdown founder Stephen Lansdown as one of its major shareholders. Lansdown was deputy chairman of the exchange until 2017.

Sabina Estates, an Ibiza property developer in which Woodford had invested, had been a particularly strong performer and it was a business he identified as one with strong long-term prospects. Listing Sabina shares on TISE would allow Woodford to remain invested in the company without breaching the regulatory quota for unlisted holdings in his main fund. The decision was taken to shift the holding onto the Guernsey exchange in 2017.

Woodford implemented the same move over the next two years for positions held in Benevolent AI. It was one of his largest unquoted holdings in Equity Income. His stakes in tech company Ombu Group and Industrial Heat were also listed in Guernsey. As the shares were technically classed as listed, the move allowed Woodford to circumvent the rules on the percentage of his fund which could hold unquoted stocks. But the decision would later come back to bite Woodford and lead to a public war of words between the Guernsey exchange and UK regulator.

III

Paul Hodges was working as an insurance analyst at Schroders in the late 1990s when he authored a piece of research that would make Neil Woodford a fortune.

There was a view that some of the world's largest tobacco manufacturers were at significant risk of litigation from individuals and local authorities who wanted to sue them to cover the cost of health care resulting from years of smoking. But the research note from Hodges claimed insurance policies taken out by tobacco giants, such as British American Tobacco, would prevent them from having to dip into the company coffers to pay out in the event of successful court claims.

Tobacco stocks, Hodges concluded, were therefore vastly undervalued.

The research was enough to convince Woodford, and so began his long-term investments in some of world's biggest cigarette manufacturers. "Hodges persuaded Woodford to buy tobacco stocks when they were on their arse. He did that and he made a fucking fortune. He's never forgotten that," says one veteran investment banker, explaining the close relationship Woodford had with Hodges. Following Schroders, Hodges went on to work at Collins Stewart as a broker, before helping to found Cenkos Securities, where he led the team responsible for helping companies list on the stock market.

Cenkos became one of Woodford's favoured brokers to do business with. It was common for the fund manager to invest large amounts in the listings Hodges and his colleagues were working on. Cenkos became a pioneer in accelerated IPOs – a process which enabled companies looking to float a much quicker route to the stock market.[53] This involved a cohort of cornerstone investors agreeing on a set price to buy a majority of a company's shares, before immediately listing it on the stock market so that other investors could become involved.

For Cenkos, having a star name like Woodford on board only served to attract interest from other large investors. While at Invesco Perpetual, Woodford backed a flurry of new company issues from Cenkos, including carbon trading group Trading Emissions and renewable energy firm Leaf Clean Energy. "Neil was the golden goose," says one former colleague of Woodford's. "From a Cenkos point of view, they could take any idea to him and he would back it. There was some of that with the unquoted. He bought the story before he bought the fundamentals."

One of the first Cenkos-led listings Woodford backed after striking out on his own from Henley was AA Group, the breakdown recovery service. Cenkos was also responsible for brokering shares in Circassia and Stobart Group – two companies Woodford bought for his Equity Income fund. But several of the listings turned out to be dire performers, with AA Group, Circassia and Stobart Group all suffering severe share price falls over a five-year period. Other companies Woodford invested in following introductions from Cenkos also tanked, including UK-based stem cell research company ReNeuron and animal health company Benchmark Holdings. Verseon, the biotech start-up which Woodford backed in 2015 after Cenkos brokered the IPO, eventually delisted from the AIM stock market after a severe drop in its share price meant the company struggled to raise funds.

Other investors have been left scratching their heads over why Woodford continued to do business with Cenkos given the success rate of the companies which they helped list. "No fund manager would ever put up with a track record like that from a broker," says one professional investor. An employment tribunal judgment handed down in January 2018 revealed just how important the Woodford connection was to Cenkos.

Cenkos employee Navid Malik, the broker's head of life sciences research, was issued a written warning by Hodges after it emerged his wife had acquired shares in a company that had just become one of its clients. This went against the company's internal policy, but Malik was not sacked. "In deciding to give [Malik] a second chance, Mr Hodges was influenced by [Malik's] relationship with an institutional investor with whom [Cenkos] worked regularly, Mr Woodford of Woodford Investment Management," the judgment said.[54]

Little did Hodges know at the time, but Malik would become a key figure in a controversy surrounding another company Woodford heavily backed called Northwest Biotherapeutics – a US-based biotech company.

Malik was a non-executive director of Northwest, a position which Cenkos allowed him to undertake. However, he failed to disclose he was also a shareholder in the company. Malik had introduced Northwest to Woodford, who later acquired a 28% stake via the Equity Income fund and Patient Capital trust. It was an investment which turned out to be another shocking bet for Woodford.

Northwest's share price nosedived in October 2015 after an anonymous group of healthcare analysts calling itself Phase Five issued a damning report on the company. Phase Five, which had an interest in lowering Northwest Bio's share price as it was shorting the company, alleged that Northwest chief executive Linda Powers had transferred company cash and shares to other entities which she controlled. Phase Five produced no evidence in its report to back up its claims, which caused Northwest Bio's share price to fall by more than 50% over a three-month period.

The debacle prompted Woodford to pile pressure on Northwest to appoint Elliott Leary, a former FBI special agent and forensic accountant, as a non-executive director to lead an inquiry into the accusations. Northwest obliged initially and met with Leary, but rejected Woodford's suggestion to appoint him having decided he did not have the necessary experience either of the pharmaceutical industry or a boardroom position. Instead Charles Price, an accountant who had also worked almost three decades at the FBI, was put in place to lead an investigation into the allegations put forward by Phase Five.

Powers denied the allegations. She said the company had

been targeted by so-called 'bear raids', orchestrated by those with an interest in lowering a company's share price with unfounded allegations.

"Such attacks have been growing in the biotech sector, as many biotech companies with valuable medical innovations are small and vulnerable," says Powers. "The claims have been extensively investigated and no evidence has ever been found to substantiate them. We have rebutted the false claims at length and in detail."

IV

Woodford's unquoted holdings had begun to attract the attention of the financial regulator.

The Financial Conduct Authority had already been in contact with Woodford's fund administrator, Link, about the two breaches of the 10% limit on unquoted holdings. Link acted as the so-called authorised corporate director for Woodford's main fund and was responsible for carrying out the valuation of unquoted assets.

The role of the ACD is an unsexy but essential role in the world of fund management. It is the ACD's role to keep a check on the individual managing a fund, ensure the interests of investors are protected, and that a fund is meeting its regulatory obligations.

In the case of Equity Income, it was Link, not Woodford, who was accountable to the FCA.

Link and the FCA have history. Before being appointed by Woodford to act as the ACD for his funds, Link (previously known as Capita Financial Managers) carried out the same oversight for two funds which went on to experience high-profile collapses, the first occurring a decade before Woodford's Equity Income fund imploded.

Thousands of investors in Arch Cru lost around £250m after the funds were suspended in 2009 following concerns about their liquidity. The funds had been touted as suitable for cautious savers, but they were invested in highly illiquid assets, including Greek shipping companies and fine wine. The scandal led to CFM paying £32m back to investors as part of a compensation scheme.

CFM also acted as the ACD for the Connaught Income fund, which collapsed in 2012. The fund, again marketed as being low risk, helped provide bridging finance to commercial operators in the UK property market. Investors lost around £118m when the fund collapsed following the liquidation of bridging loan firm Tiuta. CFM ended up paying £66m in compensation to beleaguered investors in the fund in 2017. The FCA stopped short of imposing a fine, recognising that a penalty would have meant savers in the fund would not have received back some of their investment.[55]

An investigation by the FCA concluded that when CFM took on oversight of the fund, "it did not adequately understand the structure of the fund's business or its responsibilities and duties as operator." Capita sold CFM to Australia-based Link Group in 2017 for £888m, with chief executive Chris Addenbrooke and relationship management director Karl Midl remaining with the business.[56]

Despite its previous history, Woodford pushed ahead with appointing Link when he set up his new venture in 2014. The fee for the work involved was low. "They did not make much money from this," says one former Link employee. "One of the challenges was you have competitors willing to do it for a very low number. The ACD fee has always been low for the level of responsibility required."

———————

Link had sent the FCA a breakdown of the various holdings Woodford had in his biggest fund and grouped companies into different 'buckets' depending on the length of time shares would take to sell. By the end of April 2019, 65% of assets in the Woodford Equity Income fund were invested in companies whose shares would take between 31 and more than 365 days to sell, according to the breakdown. The fund's liquidity profile had worsened from the end of June the previous year, where 55% of assets would have taken that long to sell.

But the FCA was kept in the dark about the move to list some of the fund's unquoted holdings in Guernsey. The EU rules under which Woodford's fund operated did not require him or Link to notify the FCA about the Guernsey decision, something which Andrew Bailey, the regulator's chief executive, later conceded was a flaw in the regulation. The FCA conceded it only became aware of the move after reading about it on *Citywire*, when the financial website broke the story in April 2019 that the Guernsey stock exchange had suspended the listings for Industrial Heat, Benevolent AI and Ombu over concerns about how these were being valued.

The decision by TISE to suspend the listings caused a major headache for Woodford. His Equity Income fund was now at serious risk of once again breaching the regulatory limit on unquoted holdings. The FCA later claimed it had received no contact from Guernsey about Woodford's decision to list some of his holdings on the exchange. However, in a record of correspondence between TISE and the FCA, the Guernsey exchange had tried to make initial contact with the regulator in April – only securing a meaningful telephone call a month later.

By May 2019, Woodford conceded he had to urgently address his exposure to unquoted companies and pledged to bring it below 10% by the end of the year. Woodford hoped that, in time, his largest fund would have no exposure to unlisted stocks. Any new investments in unlisted companies would be reserved for the Patient Capital trust.

There were sighs of relief at Hargreaves Lansdown, who had backed his approach. Despite Woodford having also encountered performance issues, there still signs of support from his biggest cheerleader. "Woodford's recent performance has of course been disappointing, however across a career spanning three decades, he's still delivered excellent returns for investors," said Dampier in a statement issued at the time. "This isn't the first time in his career Neil Woodford's underperformed. We've stuck with him during difficult times before, and in the past investors have been rewarded for such patience."

Unbeknown to investors, time was about to run out for Woodford.

7

Fool in the Rain

The cracks emerge

I

WOODFORD didn't know it at the time, but May 2017 would mark the high point for his business.

The Equity Income fund was the best-selling fund in the UK; assets had swelled to £10.2bn, a combination of bumper inflows having come from individual savers and large investors, as well as strong performance for companies in his portfolio. The Income Focus fund and Patient Capital Trust were also contributing to the overall success of the business. Woodford and Newman now had control of over £15bn. This sum was less than half what Woodford had overseen just before he left Invesco Perpetual, but nonetheless it was an impressive feat to be overseeing such a vast amount of money a mere three years after launching his venture.

Woodford had also started to make some bold changes to the Equity Income fund portfolio, tilting the focus towards large British companies he believed were vastly undervalued in the wake of the UK's landmark referendum vote to leave the European Union. He sold his entire position in pharmaceuticals giant GlaxoSmithKline, having lost faith in the company's long-term growth potential. The proceeds from the sale were ploughed into several domestic focused stocks including housebuilders Barratt Developments and Taylor Wimpey. One of the most significant investments made was in Lloyds Banking Group, marking Woodford's first stake in a bank since his brief dalliance with HSBC in 2014 when he set up Equity Income.

Woodford believed banks had turned a corner since the financial crisis, and was upbeat about the amount they were lending to UK businesses and the broader impact this was having on the economy. He was convinced the market had become overly cautious and pessimistic about the economic prospects following the Brexit vote – and was happy to seize on companies he thought were profoundly undervalued as a result. To some observers, Woodford was shifting Equity Income to reap the rewards of a Brexit bounce.

Woodford, who had discounted the prospect of a hard Brexit, was convinced it was only a matter of time before the stock market would receive a boost if the UK maintained a close relationship with the EU. "If Brexit pans out as I believe, we will see a long overdue and significant rally in sterling – and this will have a meaningful impact on the UK stock market," he told investors via his blog.[57] "It should at last liberate investors to start to acknowledge the underlying robust performance of the UK economy and the profound undervaluation of companies exposed to the UK economy."

Woodford should have been toasting the achievement that his Equity Income fund had broken the £10bn mark, but cracks were beginning to emerge as a string of holdings suffered performance wobbles.

———————

Allied Minds, a Boston-headquartered company which specialises in turning ideas from research labs into start-up businesses, was the first of Woodford's investments to deal a major blow to his flagship fund. The company posted an almost 30% one-day fall in April 2017 after announcing it would stop funding seven of its subsidiaries to focus on more promising business alternatives. Woodford had almost £90m invested in the company via the Equity Income fund and Patient Capital trust and suffered more than £30m paper loss after the shares crashed.

Allied Minds would deliver more bad news for Woodford four months later when it announced pre-tax losses had increased to almost $60m for the first half of 2017. Despite the value of Allied Minds shares plummeting by more than 75% over a two-year period, and at least one brokerage downgrading their expectations for the company, Woodford remained convinced it would deliver.

"In our view, Allied Minds has never been in better shape and yet its share price is pretty much as low as it ever has been in its reasonably short life thus far as a quoted business," Woodford's team told investors on its company website at the end of 2017. Allied Minds' share price would fall by almost 60% during the following year.

The sharp share price decline for Allied Minds was the start of a severely turbulent summer for Woodford, as other companies he backed made announcements that would send their share prices tumbling.

Provident Financial, a doorstep lender which specialised in providing loans and credit cards to individuals with poor credit ratings, proved to be another spectacularly poor bet for Woodford. The company lost two-thirds of its stock market value in one day during August 2017 – almost £1.7bn – after it announced a second profit warning in just two months and a cancellation of dividend payments for shareholders. Peter Crook, its CEO, also announced his resignation. The company was booted out of the FTSE 100, only having made its debut in the list of the UK's largest companies two years earlier.

To make matters worse, Provident also revealed its Vanquis Bank division was being investigated by the Financial Conduct Authority over the sale of a type of plan that allows people to freeze credit card debt. Sales of this product had provided a lucrative revenue stream for the company, worth around £70m a year. Manjit Wolstenholme, the Bradford-based company's executive chairman, took on the top job to try and steady the ship and deliver on a revamp the company had set in motion earlier in the year, including making better use of technology and cutting thousands of part-time staff who acted as debt collectors.

Woodford took to his blog to try and quell any investor concerns, telling them the market was overreacting to the profit warning and that he expected the group to post substantial profits over the next two years. "I'm not trying to dress this up as anything other than bad news – the company has given the market several reasons to be emotional," he wrote.[58] "I do, however, believe it is critically important to maintain a disciplined, fundamentally-based perspective in my investment analysis. In all situations, it is vital that I do not let emotion influence my judgement."

But Woodford's emotions would be tested to the maximum after the sudden death of Wolstenholme just three months after taking the reins. Provident's share price continued its descent. Woodford would later concede this was one investment which he had got wrong. "I'll put my hand up. This was a mistake," he told the *Financial Times* in 2019. "The company absolutely, spectacularly failed to deliver the business reorganisation that they talked to us about, at length."[59]

The experience with Provident severely tested Woodford's nerve. Unfortunately for him and his investors, it wasn't the last of its kind. A series of disastrous announcements from other investments saw the Equity Income fund continue to be severely battered.

AA Group, the roadside recovery organisation which Woodford backed during its stock market flotation, fired chief executive Bob Mackenzie in August 2017 for gross misconduct.

It later transpired that Mackenzie had been involved in a late-night hotel bar brawl with the AA's head of insurance division, Michael Lloyd. Mackenzie's departure caused AA's share price to drop by almost 20% in one day, wiping £200m from the company's value. The company had more bad news to deliver six months later, when it announced its profits for 2019 would fall some £55m short of analyst expectations because of the huge sums it was investing in new technology to alert drivers to potential breakdowns before they happen. The news sent AA's share price down by 28%. The news delivered a big hit to Woodford: his Equity Income fund was one of the company's largest shareholders.

Prothena, a US-based biotechnology company which Woodford heavily backed via all three of his funds, was the next investment to cause the stock picker a major headache. The company's share price tumbled by almost 70% after it announced it would stop further research into a treatment for amyloidosis after a failed trial into the rare disease, which causes a build up of an abnormal protein in tissues and organs in the human body.

It was not the first time a failed drugs trial had burned Woodford. Circassia, an Oxford-based pharmaceuticals company which counted the fund manager as its largest investor, saw its shares drop by almost two-thirds in a day in June 2016 after it announced the failure of a trial for a cat-allergy treatment. The drug trial, which was being conducted on people with a severe allergic reaction to cats, showed a placebo had broadly the same impact on symptoms – a factor Woodford described as "unprecedented" in earlier studies on Circassia's cat allergy product or any of its other potential allergy treatments.

Some of Woodford's colleagues were harbouring concerns about his investments in such specialist companies, not least because these were becoming bigger players in his main fund which was a big hit among retail savers. "You need to be an arsehole in that game," says a former colleague of Woodford's. "The people you are up against are teams of PhDs in biochemistry with US institutional backing. You should not be putting that in a product that is sold to the retail market. It's completely wrong."

Woodford played down the severe drop in the company's share price, telling investors that he continued to see long-term value. Woodford's support for the company did not come as a huge surprise. Steven Harris, Circassia's chief executive, was a member of the board of the Patient Capital trust.

Even some of the best-known stocks Woodford had backed were beginning to test his patience. AstraZeneca's shares dropped by more than 15% in one day during July 2017 and wiped £10bn from its market value after the pharmaceuticals giant said a trial for a new lung cancer drug had failed. It was the biggest one day fall in shares for the company. The project, dubbed Mystic, was regarded as key to AstraZeneca's long-term growth.

Imperial Brands, the tobacco company in which Woodford had remained loyally invested since his Invesco Perpetual days, was also encountering performance issues. Between late 2016 and mid-2019, company shares fell more than 50% as a result of changing attitudes towards smoking coupled with growing competition from e-cigarettes and vaping products. Although Imperial had produced vaping products, questions about the long-term health implications had cast a shadow over the long-term profitability of the sector.

Just when things couldn't get any worse for the fund manager, outsourcing company Capita issued a profit warning at the start of 2018 which caused shares to plummet 40%. Woodford was a top five shareholder in the company and had no plans to turn his back on it anytime soon. "I am not trying to make a silk purse out of a sow's ear – this has been a poor investment, but it is one that has the capacity to become a significantly better one from here," he wrote on his blog the day after shares collapsed. Just eight months later, Woodford sold his entire stake in Capita, ending a relationship with the company going back to 2003.

Purple Bricks, the online estate agent which Woodford had backed before the company had listed, also punished Woodford. The company posted a share price drop of more than 20% in February 2019 after disappointing results for its businesses in Australia and the US. The CEO of its UK business and the boss of its US operation also announced their departures.

Woodford's performance was now tanking. He was facing a crisis unlike any other he had encountered in his career.

II

"I would be doing you, my investors, a massive injustice if I was to abandon the investment discipline that has guided me for 30 years in this industry," Woodford told investors following the Capita share price drop.

With investors nursing painful losses as a result of a long line of disastrous stock picks, some of Woodford's colleagues were beginning to question whether he had lost it. The real problem was that Woodford was unwilling to change. "His approach to investing and the level of detail and due diligence he thought was sufficient and robust in the 1980s and 1990s, was enough to get results," says a former employee who worked with Woodford. "But the market is more sophisticated today. The competition evolved significantly over the three decades he'd been running funds – he stuck to what he knew. There was a degree of complacency because he was so long term."

By the end of 2017, investors had pulled almost £2bn from the Equity Income fund. Not all of them were ordinary savers. Jupiter, which had jumped at the chance of investing with Woodford when he launched his new venture, was the first big client to bail on the fund manager, pulling £300m from the fund in September 2017. The firm, which invested in Equity Income via a suite of its own funds, had been a client of Woodford's for around 20 years, having backed him during his time at Invesco. It put £660m into Equity Income when the fund was launched in June 2014, topping up its investment with another £150m three months later.

But it had become increasingly concerned about Woodford's investment in unquoted companies and by 2015 had started to unwind the investment it had amassed in the flagship fund. "In November 2015 we started to take our investment out as we began to have concerns with the fund," says John Chatfeild-Roberts, who oversees the team which runs Jupiter's Merlin fund range.

During the next 12 months, Chatfeild-Roberts and his team sat down with Woodford and his analysts over and above the normal six-monthly cycle it would usually meet with fund managers. "We were getting concerned," says the veteran City investor, who had noticed a change in the way Woodford spoke about some of his investments. "Woodford used to be very on it in terms of knowing the detail about his stocks, the forecasts and numbers. He started becoming very general and directing the conversation onto companies we'd not heard of. His attention was obviously being diverted and over time we made the decision to get out."

Chatfeild-Roberts could see the liquidity problems Woodford's fund was heading towards, and sold down Jupiter's holding consistently over 2016 and the first three quarters of 2017, offloading chunks of between £5m and £64m per deal. "It wasn't a case of ringing up and asking for £1bn in one go," he says. Chatfeild-Roberts says the fund had become more heavily exposed to unquoted companies than Jupiter would have expected.

"Were we misled? We certainly misunderstood at the start the extent of what he was going to do in the unquoted sector," he says. "We expected him to up the ante on unquoteds a little, but didn't expect it to be much different to what he did previously at Invesco. When he launched the fund he held six unquoteds; that number was 45 by the time we exited."

Weeks after Jupiter's announcement, UK insurer Aviva said

it was shelving the Equity Income fund from an investment platform used by pension investors, a decision which would see £30m pulled from the fund manager. Woodford was beginning to look vulnerable.

If severe stock price falls weren't enough to cause serious headaches for Woodford, investment platforms were also starting to turn their backs on him as performance of his largest fund dropped off a cliff.

In May 2018 investment platform Charles Stanley ditched Equity Income from its list of favoured funds after it had been on there for almost three and a half years. Explaining its decision to clients, Charles Stanley's investment analyst Rob Morgan said it had begun to "harbour concerns" that overall performance of the fund may be impacted by the number of early-stage businesses Woodford had invested in. AJ Bell, another online stockbroker, followed suit four months later by removing Woodford's largest fund from its list of most favoured investments. The move by both platforms was at odds with Hargreaves Lansdown, which continued to promote Woodford's fund among its list of best investment picks.

By this point the financial press had latched onto a potential story about a star fund manager losing his Midas touch. With each negative press article came another wave of outflows from Woodford's flagship fund. Woodford would later blame some of the negative attention he'd received for the large outflows, claiming investors were being led to make "appallingly bad decisions" by "misinformation and lazy commentary".

"There is a mountain of fake information and fake analysis out in the marketplace which, in the end, does impact investors' decisions detrimentally. So, that's what pisses me off," he said in a *Financial Times* interview three months before his fund was suspended.[60] "When you passionately believe in what you're doing, as I do, when clients are saying, 'nah, we want our money back now because we'd much rather be investing in these things that have gone up', that, for me, is a frustration. I think they're making a poor investment decision."

One former employee at a large investor which pulled money from Woodford's Equity Income fund says it was getting more and more uncomfortable with performance, as well as the number of compliance officers that had walked away from the business. "Nobody wanted to say they were selling out for those reasons," he says. "Investors were saying the investment style was out of favour, but the real reasons were risk management and governance."

Some of Woodford's largest investors were afraid of speaking out and offending the fund manager, fearing they would not be able to get back into the fund on favourable terms. "They weren't foreseeing the collapse, but they were afraid of speaking out against him," says the former investor. "There was so much nervousness about it."

There were also mounting questions about the string of key risk and compliance personnel Woodford was working his way through. Following the departure of Woodford's first risk and compliance head Gray Smith just months after the business was set up, there was a succession of replacements. The company hired Gavin St John-Heath and Simon Osborne in the wake of Smith's abrupt departure, with the duo taking on risk and compliance roles. But St John-Heath left after just eight months in the job and Osborne walked in 2017 having been at the firm for less than three years.

"Nick Hamilton and Gray Smith were visibly not happy," says a former Woodford Investment Management employee, adding that not all those with compliance duties to fulfil after the duo left appeared as concerned to challenge the fund manager. "There was a huge investment shift from Invesco to Woodford, but it was justified and it was exciting. We launched Patient Capital to give people more exposure to that. Unfortunately he has been dreadfully unlucky or not managed it properly," says the former staffer. "There was an overriding optimism that the business would continue to gather money and would never have to give it back. If you had more experienced people in compliance, they might have said 'no you can't do that.' But the business was set up to give Neil the freedom to do things."

Outsiders also began to question some of Woodford's investment choices.

Peter Sleep, a senior portfolio manager at Seven Investment Management, had taken a look at some of Woodford's holdings when he was still managing money at Invesco Perpetual. Even during that time there were some obvious red flags, says the former chartered accountant. "He had massive holdings of listed companies, 20% or 30% that would take ages to sell. They may appear to be liquid companies but when you've got 30% of a company they're anything but liquid," says Sleep.

Sleep attributes a lot of Woodford's success to the sheer weight of money he had invested in some of the small and mid-sized companies he backed during his career. "When you buy 30% of a company, you're going to push the share price up, and then when you start selling it, you're going to take a lot of the air out of the stock price," says Sleep.

Morningstar, which rates funds on a five-point spectrum ranging from negative to gold, also had bad news for Woodford. Analysts at the company had become increasingly concerned about some of the poor performance and the way Woodford was positioning his investments. As a result, it decided to downgrade the Woodford Equity Income fund from bronze to neutral – just one notch above its negative rating.

Morningstar analyst Peter Brunt went straight in for the kill. He claimed "persistent redemptions, underperformance and stock-specific issues, combined with [Woodford's] relentless willingness to push the portfolio to its liquidity limit, have resulted in portfolio positioning that we consider extreme."

Woodford's largest fund was on its knees.

With £4.4bn in assets, it was shrinking at an alarming rate and was now less than half the size it was at its peak two years previously. Most of Woodford's largest clients had deserted him and thousands of retail investors were clinging on to the hope Hargreaves Lansdown and other Woodford supporters would be right in predicting he could turn around performance.

8

In My Time of Dying

The crisis hits

I

BARRY LEWIS had a hunch that Woodford's winning streak would one day come to an abrupt end. The former bookmaker became a Labour councillor for Margate in 2017 and immediately began to question the fees Woodford was charging the Kent County Council pension fund as his fund's performance began to nosedive.

"As a gambler, you know if you back three winners on the trot the fourth one will lose to bring down the average," says Lewis, known as 'Bolshy Barry' to fellow councillors for his dogged approach. "If someone is making such a high percentage, it's too good to be true to last any length of time. If you back a horse at 10/1 you don't keep backing it until it goes down to 2/1."

Members of Kent County Council's superannuation committee, who made the investment decisions on behalf of the pension scheme, had found a formidable opponent.

Kent County Council was one of Woodford's most loyal clients, having invested with the fund manager during his time at Invesco Perpetual, where it had entrusted around £200m on behalf of its pension fund. The relationship with the council went from strength to strength as Woodford delivered exceptional returns. The value of Kent's investment with the fund manager while he was at Invesco grew to almost £400m in 2012 and reached a peak of £530m in 2014.[61]

Like thousands of individual investors who followed Woodford to his new business, Kent had enough confidence that the fund manager could deliver equally impressive returns; it funnelled £216m into the Equity Income fund without hesitation.

But three years on, pension fund committee members had started to get anxious about Woodford's bout of poor performance. They wanted some assurance from him personally that it would improve.

There was a certain amount of pressure on Kent County Council, as it did not have the best investment track record.

On 30 September 2008, back when Woodford was still a rockstar fund manager making all the right calls, an urgent email had been sent to a junior member of staff at Kent County Council's headquarters in Maidstone. The message contained vital information about the credit worthiness of Iceland's largest banks. They were on the verge of collapse.

Kent County Council had around £50m sitting in Icelandic banks, investments which had been made to take advantage of the market-beating interest rates being offered at the time. More than 120 councils had made similar deposits – but Kent's was the single largest amount held by any UK local authority.

Iceland's banks were in serious trouble. The financial crisis had just hit, and three of the country's biggest lenders – Glitner, Landsbanki and Kaupthing – were unable to refinance their short-term debt following the collapse of Lehman Brothers in September 2008. US and UK banks were also left teetering on the edge. The US government moved to approve a $700bn bailout package for some of the biggest banks on Wall Street; the UK government pledged £500bn to rescue some of Britain's best-known high-street lenders. Iceland's government took a different approach, refusing to stump up the enormous sums needed to keep its banks afloat. Instead, it let them fail.

Kent had money tied up in all three of Iceland's biggest banks, which were now on the brink of collapse. The major rating agencies had been steadily downgrading these banks over several months, and other local pension funds had begun to pull their money after spotting the warning signs. A report by the Audit Commission in 2009 branded Kent County Council and six other local authorities negligent for failing to spot the warning signs about investing in Icelandic banks days before they toppled.

The email sent to the junior member of staff went unnoticed. Kent County Council proceeded to plough more than £3m into Heritable, a UK subsidiary of Landsbanki. Days later, the bank collapsed.

II

A crunch meeting between Kent County Council and Woodford was called for December 2017 where superannuation committee chairman, Conservative councillor Charlie Simkins, would meet Woodford to discuss his recent bout of poor performance and get him to explain where it had all gone wrong.

Minutes from a previous committee meeting laid bare the council's concerns. Committee members were rattled by some of the sharp share price falls that had dealt a blow to Woodford's largest fund, in particular the steep decline posted by Provident Financial.

"The recent problems have had extensive media coverage and there have been some high-profile investments which have gone badly wrong, Provident being notable," the documents said. "Neil Woodford's investment approach is not benchmark constrained, and there can be significant under- and over-performance."

Lewis says he had begun putting questions to the pension fund committee about Kent County Council's investment with Woodford, in particular the fees that were being levied during a period of such poor performance. Kent County Council paid more than £20m in investment management fees in 2019, although not all of this went to Woodford. Some councillors were wondering whether the investment in Woodford represented value for money, given the poor performance.

The investment mandate handed to Woodford made up around 5% of the pension scheme's overall assets, but compared to other fund managers with which Kent had large investments, his performance stuck out like a sore thumb. In the final financial year before the fund was suspended, pension fund investments overseen by UBS, Goldman Sachs, Kames and Fidelity all matched or comfortably exceeded their benchmarks. Woodford's performance was the only one in the red.

Lewis claims any questions he put to the committee were met with silence. "It was too cosy an arrangement. It seemed like a cosy club divorced from the rest of Kent County Council," he says.

Pension funds are complex to oversee, with committees made up of regular company employees with no expert investment knowledge. The job can be overwhelming; those with committee roles are expected to decide where to invest hundreds of millions of pounds on behalf of retirees or those still paying into the scheme. Put simply, their job is to invest money with the purpose of maximising returns for scheme members. In the case of Kent County Council, it is one of the largest pension schemes in the UK with around 150,000 members and £6.6bn in assets. Committee members rely on assistance and guidance from professional investment advisers, often large companies that act as a sort of matchmaker between pension schemes and fund managers. Hymans Robertson acted as investment advisers to Kent County Council when Woodford was appointed in 2014 but was later replaced by Mercer. Often large investors with hundreds of millions of pounds to invest with a fund manager will opt for a separate pocket to place their investment, known as a segregated mandate. This approach prevents pension fund investments being diluted with retail savers and allows them to call more of the shots, such as placing a limit on certain types of investments and pulling cash without affecting others. But all this comes at a greater cost. Kent County Council was lumped together with hundreds of thousands of others in Woodford's Equity Income fund, putting the hundreds of millions it had invested at the same risk as individual savers with a few thousand pounds.

The approach taken by Kent did not go unnoticed. John Ralfe, a pension fund expert, says schemes with tens of millions of pounds at their disposal would typically approach a fund manager via their investment adviser and negotiate the terms under which they invest in a retail fund. "It's not to say it isn't done. But in terms of good practice, it looks very odd," says Ralfe. "The corporate governance within local government pension schemes is absolutely dreadful. The people usually in charge of making decisions haven't got a clue, and like the idea of having money to play with. But they are reliant on advisers."

At the meeting with council officials, Woodford did enough to convince them he was worth keeping. But he failed to turn around performance and continued to lose substantial amounts of money for Kent County Council. By the end of

2018, the council's investment with the fund manager stood at £255m, significantly less than the £317m it had been worth in March 2017. Performance was dire. By the end of May 2019 Woodford's Equity Income fund had lost investors 17% over a three-year period, compared to the FTSE All Share index which had returned a positive 28.44%.[62]

By this point Woodford's main fund had also shrunk significantly in size, now down to £3.71bn.

Pension fund committee members again began to voice concerns about their earlier decision to stick by Woodford. In council meeting minutes, committee members expressed alarm over "the adverse publicity associated with Woodford" but said they would keep the mandate under review. The matter would be discussed when the committee met with Woodford three months later. But then, as it happened, the meeting never took place.

Council members had had enough and convened to discuss the options for redeeming their investment. On 31 May, they voted to pull their money from Woodford's fund with immediate effect.

III

The job of breaking the bad news to Woodford and his team fell to Nick Vickers, the head of financial services at Kent County Council, who had been a close contact of Woodford's during the time the local authority had money invested in his Invesco funds.

Woodford and his team were told the decision was irreversible.

The talks took place behind closed doors in County Hall and there was a strict no-press policy. Any decisions made were done so without opportunity for committee members to be challenged or held to account at a later date. Martin Whybrow, another local Kent councillor, says: "There was no transparency around the decision making. The presentation from Woodford to the committee members was only a few months before everything went pear shaped, but we have no audit trail. It's a key failure."

Kent County Council's own audit committee later produced a scathing report about how pension fund committee members dealt with the investment in Woodford's fund. Despite being able to call on the help of its investment advisers, the report claimed the committee was heavily influenced by what it had read in press reports about Woodford and his drop in performance. It also chastised committee members for failing to commission any independent investment advice from Mercer when reviewing the investment in Woodford's fund.

Sensing the impending damage Kent's bombshell announcement would cause as yet another large investor fled his fund, Woodford's team suggested the local authority withdraw its money in stages to soften the blow.

As the fund's administrator, Link was also growing increasingly anxious. It fired questions to Woodford's team about how such a large redemption might impact the fund's ability to meet withdrawal requests from other investors, particularly if Kent stuck by its decision to pull all its money in one go and reject the idea for an 'in-specie transfer'.

This option would have allowed assets in the fund to be transferred to Kent County Council to match the size of its current investment, preventing Woodford from having to sell shares in companies to raise the money to pay the council.

But Kent was standing firm with its original decision.

9

Heartbreaker

The lock in

I

CRAIG NEWMAN was in shock. He had just come off a regular Monday morning call with Karl Midl, Link's managing director, and was now rushing to Woodford's office to deliver his business partner the worst possible news.

The crucial telephone call had not gone the way Newman had expected. The bombshell he was about to drop would send the business into a tailspin.

Woodford's closest advisers had spent a fraught weekend putting together a plan of action to discuss with Midl during the call, which would show how the Equity Income fund could comfortably manage Kent County Council's request to pull the plug. The local authority had been sending signals for weeks that it was planning to ditch Woodford at a meeting it had lined up with the fund manager on 21 June.

Kent County Council had given Woodford plenty of chances to turn around his ailing performance but he had simply failed to deliver and was losing them millions of pounds. Enough was enough.

Midl emailed Woodford's team over the weekend asking what would happen if Kent wanted its money back in one go and the impact such a quick exit might have on the fund's ability to pay other investors wanting to leave. Newman planned to tell Midl the fund had enough cash to deal with the worst-case scenario, and that Woodford would offload shares in certain companies over the coming weeks to raise enough cash to boost liquidity.

Woodford had accepted Kent County Council was about to leave. But with his fund bleeding around £100m a month by this point, he had to prepare for the event that even heavier outflows were a possibility, as hordes of ordinary savers reacted to news that another big client had walked out on him.

But Newman and the rest of Woodford's team never got the chance to follow through with their plans. Link shocked them all with its decision to suspend the Equity Income fund – a move considered to be in the best interests of investors.

———

Fund suspensions are rare but they are a useful tool that open-ended funds can use in extreme conditions and when they face periods where investors are looking to exit en masse. In 2016, when the UK voted to leave the European Union, some of the largest British property funds were forced to close the gates after nervous investors began to pull hundreds of millions of pounds over fears that Brexit would hit the country's commercial real estate sector. The onset of the Covid-19 crisis prompted British property funds to suspend once again, as the companies responsible for pricing the real estate in which these funds invest were unable to provide accurate valuations given severe market uncertainty.

The announcement from Midl left Woodford and Newman dumbfounded. A suspension was not an option they were led to believe was being considered during their communications with Link over the weekend.

Kent County Council's long-standing relationship with Woodford would be over in just a few hours. To make matters worse, Woodford's main contact at the council, Nick Vickers, was away on holiday for the rest of the week. Kent's official redemption request came through in the first data file of the morning at Woodford's headquarters, and his team had just one hour to process it before a trading cut-off deadline of midday.

But the local authority was in for a big surprise.

At 4.25pm officials at County Hall in Maidstone received a phone call from Woodford's team breaking the news: it was now trapped in the fund with no clear indication when it might get its money back.

II

Woodford looked dreadful. Tired and withdrawn, he had arrived early to the office on the morning of 4 June to deal with the firestorm engulfing his business. It had been a whirlwind 24 hours. Only a couple of months before, Woodford had lambasted the media in a newspaper interview for the role he believed they played in making matters worse for his fund. Now he was front-page news.

With emotions running high, Woodford refused to field any questions from journalists up and down the UK who were eager to get the next instalment in one of the most sensational stories they had ever covered.

Following Link's surprise announcement, a press statement was rushed out to explain how the suspension would initially last 28 days to allow Woodford enough time to "reposition" his Equity Income fund by selling shares in some of the smaller companies he owned and ploughing the proceeds into bigger, more liquid stocks.

It was a PR nightmare that Woodford had to deal with fast.

———————

A downbeat Woodford was sitting in the foyer of his office. Two video cameras were trained on his slumped figure. They had been set up for him to film an apology he hoped would placate thousands of angry investors who now found themselves locked in his fund with no way of accessing their savings.

Hunched forwards, Woodford was visibly uncomfortable as he gathered his thoughts and prepared to speak down the camera lens. He refused to put on a shirt and tie, even when explaining what had happened to his clients' money, opting for his trademark casual sweater and jeans.

The short video would be uploaded onto Woodford's YouTube channel, which he had used to communicate with investors since setting up the business. The video updates were another way Woodford set himself apart from some of his larger, stuffier rivals, and were in keeping with the digital vibe his new business was trying to portray.

Not all the videos posted on Wooodford's channel were meant to be about investment. Some were meant to bring out Woodford's personality, including a light-hearted series called 'Awkward corner' where viewers could ask the fund manager whatever they wanted. A few of the questions posed just two years previously turned out to be foreboding, including "Is there anyone at Woodford challenging Neil's decisions?" and "Has Neil Woodford lost it?"

The relaxed videos of Woodford smirking as he read out some of the submissions were a far cry from the solemn message he was now getting ready to deliver. During his time at Invesco, Woodford had navigated the dotcom bubble and financial crash and had proved his doubters wrong. This time he had to convince the naysayers that he had what it took to deliver a miraculous comeback.

The video lasted just three minutes, but it felt like an eternity for Woodford. "I'm extremely sorry that we've had to take this decision," he told investors, assuring them the move was in their best interests and that it would allow him to build a portfolio which would leave the fund in a better position. "We understand our investors' frustration."

Woodford's direct message did little to calm furious investors, who could scarcely believe that one of the UK's most lauded fund managers was now telling them they no longer had access to their savings. Many now clung onto the hope Woodford would be able to dramatically turn things around to enable the fund to re-open in a few weeks.

Among them was Mike Cox, a retired financial services worker from Tunbridge Wells, who initially ploughed £28,000 into Woodford's Equity Income fund, topping this up with regular monthly sums. Investments made by Cox and his wife into the fund totalled £40,000 by the time it was suspended.

"At the time I thought 'Oh, bollocks'," says Cox, recalling when he first heard the fund had been suspended. "I didn't worry about it too much because his reputation seemed to suggest that things would all be good over the long term. It never occurred to me that a fund with his name on it would utterly collapse."

The fund suspension had dealt Woodford an almighty blow. And just as he was preparing to pull himself off the ropes, another monumental crisis was on its way to deliver the knockout punch.

Once Newman and Woodford had a chance to digest the surprise announcement from Link, employees working in the Oxford office were hauled into a meeting room where they were briefed about what had just happened.

Woodford and Newman put on brave faces as they addressed colleagues.

"It was a massive surprise to a lot of people", says one employee present in the meeting. "But people were resolute. We all thought it was something that had been imposed on us and we would just roll up our sleeves and deal with it. There wasn't a sense of panic at that point".

The level-headedness displayed by Woodford and Newman was about to be severely tested. The business partners had only just got over the shock of the fund suspension when another of Woodford's most faithful clients sprung a last-minute surprise.

St James's Place had been one of Woodford's first backers when he launched his new business in 2014, handing him the keys to a suite of funds worth a collective £3.5bn. The business relationship was structured as a segregated mandate, which enabled St James's Place to keep a check on some of the investment decisions being made on behalf of its funds. Crucially, it had requested Woodford not to make any bets on unquoted companies and only invest in FTSE 100 and FTSE 250 stocks.

The decision may have saved it from being trapped in the Equity Income fund with Kent County Council, but performance was still woeful. The SJP UK High Income fund, which Woodford oversaw on behalf of the wealth manager, had lost investors more than 17% over a two-year period.

St James's Place had been delivering mixed messages in the week leading up to it ditching the fund manager. In an interview with the *FT* its chief investment officer Chris Ralph said it was "intently focused" on Woodford's recent performance, giving the impression that it was considering its options.[63] Four days later, St James's Place issued a statement to confirm its support for Woodford, saying the wealth manager had "no plans to change his mandate."

But St James's Place had been conducting conversations behind Woodford's back and had already lined up two other City asset management firms – Columbia Threadneedle and RWC – to take over the funds Woodford had been managing for the past five years.

St James's Place disowned Woodford and dumped him in the most spectacular fashion, notifying the fund manager of its decision while simultaneously announcing the news to its clients. As one of Woodford's former colleagues put it: "St James's Place was just another example of someone saying 'fuck you'."

III

Hargreaves Lansdown had spent months defending its decision to keep Woodford's failing Equity Income fund on its prestigious list of preferred products. But the time had come. It could no longer stand by him.

Despite claiming its internal research process ensured only the very best fund managers made it onto its buy list, there was no formal metric it used for deciding when to cull them. Instead, a struggling fund manager's place was determined by how much faith Hargreaves Lansdown's research team had in his or her ability to turn around bouts of poor performance.

The company received more scrutiny when it overhauled the Wealth 150 list at the start of 2019, reducing the number of funds to between 50 and 60 in order to declutter the line-up. That had been the perfect chance to quietly ditch Woodford. Instead, it chose to stick by him yet again.

Woodford had delivered impressive results for more than two years after launching his flagship fund in 2014 and Hargreaves Lansdown was still expecting great things from him. Gating the fund now potentially ruined those chances. With investors unable to invest in Woodford's flagship fund, the decision to pull it from the overhauled buy-list was, at long last, a no-brainer.

The move would have dire consequences for Woodford. Hargreaves Lansdown also announced his smaller Income Focus fund – then still open for dealing – was to be dropped from its coveted list. Hargreaves Lansdown said it wanted to see the dealing suspension lifted on Woodford's main fund before coming to a final decision on whether its sister fund should also keep its place.

The research team in Bristol also recognised that this was its opportunity to overhaul its approach to how it selected which managers made the cut. By now, its buy list had become the subject of intense scrutiny. One of the first changes implemented by Dampier and his team was to focus on the media profiles of individual fund managers. Journalists had given Woodford a rough ride, with outflows from his fund coinciding with some of the most negative press coverage. Hargreaves Lansdown could not afford the same thing to happen to other high-profile individuals it had thrown its support behind. It decided it was time to take a closer look at some of the coverage they were generating.

The contagion had already begun to spread to Woodford's other funds. Nervous investors had yanked more than £100m from the smaller Income Focus in the week after Equity Income was gated, with the outflows led by Hargreaves Lansdown – who pulled £45m it had invested via its multi-manager funds.

The much smaller Patient Capital trust was also beginning to suffer, with its share price dropping by almost 25% in the month after Equity Income was gated as investors began to question if Woodford would be sacked as its manager.

Crucially, Hargreaves Lansdown said it would waive its fees for those investors left trapped in the fund. The move would later cost it around £2.6m in lost revenue, but it was piling pressure on Woodford to do the same while the fund remained suspended. Woodford, however, refused to budge.

Behind the scenes, and realising what was at stake, Hargreaves Lansdown took a lead in trying to find a solution to rescue Woodford's biggest fund. It approached Aberdeen Standard Investments, an Edinburgh-headquartered asset manager, to see if there was a way it could salvage Equity Income. Hargreaves Lansdown worked with a team of lawyers to devise a plan.

The proposal was for Aberdeen Standard Investments to take on Woodford's suspended fund along with the Patient Capital trust, given the crossover with some holdings. Assets across Equity Income and the Patient Capital trust would have been split into a 'good bank/bad bank'-like structure based on their individual liquidity profile. This would have allowed a fund containing the most liquid holdings to be re-opened, giving savers the option to remain invested or redeem their holdings.

It was a potential way forward, and one that Hargreaves and Aberdeen Standard Investments argued would avoid a fire sale of holdings. It would also provide a lifeline to Hargreaves Lansdown clients, but it was an approach that would have seen Woodford sacked as manager.

The plan was put to Link, who assessed it on several merits including the speed of giving investors access to their savings and the ability for investors to easily understand the process. Having failed to meet Link's strict criteria, the plan was swiftly rejected.

IV

Woodford's week of woes was far from over. The Financial Conduct Authority said it had started to examine his decision to list some of unquoted companies on the Guernsey stock exchange, threatening to open an investigation if it found any evidence of serious misconduct or non-compliance.

In a television interview with Bloomberg two days after the fund was suspended, FCA chief executive (now governor of the Bank of England) Andrew Bailey signalled his support for gating it. "The reason it was necessary and essential there was a suspension of the fund, is otherwise you could have had a disorderly process of investors exiting," he said.[64] "Investors will say that has restricted my options. I would counter that by saying the alternative would have been much more disorderly."

It was the first time Bailey acknowledged there could be a potential problem with funds like Woodford's, which invested in illiquid assets but also had to ensure they had the ability to pay back investors wanting to make an exit. "Ten years ago we were dealing with the problem of banks that were too big to fail. Of course, we don't want funds that are too big to fail," Bailey said during the Bloomberg interview.

Woodford had now lost two of his big backers just a few days apart from each other. Clients that had fallen over themselves to get through the front door of Woodford's new business five years earlier now wanted nothing to do with him.

Sensing trouble ahead, Woodford's staff began to worry about their futures. The can-do attitude that had existed across the office just two days previously, when the suspension had been first announced, was quickly replaced by one of heightened anxiety.

For the second time in a week, Woodford and Newman told employees to gather in a conference room where they were warned of potential tough times ahead. Talks about cost cutting and headcount reductions would need to be had, they were told. The staff who had joined Woodford's business five years earlier couldn't believe what they were hearing. Rather than continuing to ride the wave of optimism, the future was beginning to look extremely bleak.

"Losing St James's Place had a big financial impact on the business. A huge chunk of revenue walked out in one day and people started to think 'Shit, this isn't good'," says one former worker. "It was the first time people started to question whether this was a viable business."

10

No Quarter

The backlash

I

FIVE years after the most successful fund launch in British history, Woodford's eponymous business empire was now deep in crisis and fighting for survival. Investors who had closely followed Woodford throughout his almost 30-year career could hardly believe the drama that was unfolding.

The unexpected fund suspension had caused some investors to point the finger of blame at Kent County Council for requesting such a huge investment back as one single payment. But, unable to access its multi-million pound investment, the local authority publicly hit back at Woodford and the decision to gate the fund, claiming it had no idea its actions would lead to paralysis for other investors.

"KCC is disappointed that, as a major investor in the fund, we did not receive this prior notification," the council said. Woodford was summoned to Maidstone weeks later to meet with angry pension fund committee members to explain what had happened. But trying to placate Kent County Council was the least of Woodford's problems.

It didn't take long before the tabloid newspapers latched onto the story and began to profile some of the thousands of ordinary savers who were locked in the struggling fund. Once lauded by the press as the man who made Middle England rich, Woodford was now being portrayed as the pantomime villain, accused of holding people hostage in his fund as he continued to rake in tens of thousands of pounds a day in fees.

Investors were referred to as "prisoners" and "victims" and started to contact journalists to provide personal stories about how they were having to cancel holidays and pause house renovations, and were incurring sleepless nights with worry.

Whatever dwindling faith investors had left in Woodford to salvage performance completely evaporated when Link announced the initial 28-day suspension period would be extended for at least another month.

Woodford once again took to social media to post another video update, this time seated at an almost empty desk, save for a couple of computer screens with stock tickers flashing red and green in the background. With his hands clasped tightly, some of the strain evident on his face during his previous video update had vanished.

Wooodford vowed to use the time he had to diversify the fund's portfolio by investing in FTSE 100 and FTSE 250 stocks, but stressed any changes would still be aligned with his approach of picking the most undervalued companies he believed offered the greatest potential for growth. Woodford might have to back away from some of the smaller companies he felt still offered great growth potential, but he needed to ensure he had left his mark on the fund.

Ironically, Woodford's desire when setting up his business to be fully transparent by providing a full list of his portfolio holdings had started to work against him. As performance of the Equity Income continued to tank, other large investors could spot which companies the fund manager would have to offload in order to increase liquidity in his fund.

Hedge funds were now taking out short positions in companies they knew Woodford might have to sell, hoping their share prices would drop enough for them to make a quick profit at his expense.

Rival fund managers had also begun to circle some of Woodford's existing holdings in the hope they could snap them up at a discount as he desperately sought to offload them.

The fund was in a death spiral.

II

To maintain some of the share prices at companies still invested by the fund, Woodford took the decision to impose a partial blackout on holdings, limiting the information to just the top ten companies in the portfolio. However, he was forced to stop providing even this limited information as he struggled not to sell shares at a huge discount.

Woodford desperately needed more time to get a handle on the situation; Link informed investors at the end of July that the fund would remain suspended until the end of the year.

By the end of August, performance had worsened for the fund – down nearly 15% over a three-month period and almost 34% on a three-year basis. With no investor money able to leave the fund, continued poor performance of existing holdings and the fact Woodford was selling down stakes meant assets had shrivelled to just £3.1bn.

By now, savers were losing their patience and beginning to wonder if the fund would ever re-open. Anger was also starting to boil over about Woodford's reluctance to stop charging fees while his fund was closed. The earlier pleas from Hargreaves Lansdown for Woodford to follow their lead and waive charges while the fund was shuttered had fallen on deaf ears.

It was easy to understand why investors were up in arms. Woodford and Newman had pocketed £36.5m between them during the previous financial year, bringing the total amount they had paid themselves in dividends since establishing the business to more than £95m.

Newman, who was described as the "driving force" behind Woodford's business on the company website, seemed to be keeping a low profile as the crisis was playing out. It might have been Woodford's name above the door, but Newman was still chief executive of the business and some were expecting him to step up.[65] Unfortunately for Newman, he was thrown into the spotlight when documents were leaked to *The Times* about two property sales he was trying to push through while the fund was suspended.

Like Woodford, Newman had an interest in acquiring sprawling country estates and had spent millions refurbishing a seven-bedroom Arts and Crafts-style country house near Henley-on-Thames, which Newman bought in 2015 just as his new venture with Woodford was attracting billions of pounds from investors.

The work carried out on Harpsden Wood House took more than four years and included installing an orangery, a summer house, tennis court, swimming pool, stables and gatehouse as well as completely renovating the gardens.

Having toiled to completely overhaul the property, built in 1908 by a protégé of Sir Edwin Lutyens, Newman was looking to sell it for £10m.[66] Meanwhile he was also looking to offload a six-bedroom property he built himself at nearby Wargrave in Berkshire for £4.85m.

There was some speculation that Newman was in a rush to sell the properties to build a legal warchest to fight any potential legal action from angry investors in future – a claim strenuously denied by Woodford's spokesman at the time.

Having raked in tens of millions in fees over the past five years, and with a bulging personal property portfolio, investors had little sympathy for Woodford and Newman.

The business was still pulling in £65,000 a day in fee revenue, with estimates that more than £10m would have been collected between the fund's suspension in June and the end of the year. It was a slap in the face to ordinary savers.[67]

In his defence, Woodford argued that continuing to charge fees was necessary while the fund was closed as making changes to the portfolio incurred certain costs. There were overheads that still had to be met. But it didn't wash with investors or the growing chorus of senior political figures who now voiced their own concerns.

Nicky Morgan, chair of parliament's influential Treasury select committee at the time Woodford's fund was suspended, was among the high-profile figures urging him to do the right thing. "The unfairness that people felt at paying fees while they couldn't get their money out runs through a lot of this," Morgan recalls. "People will accept many things, but not unfairness."

Bailey got involved once again, telling BBC Radio 4's *Today* programme that Woodford should "consider his position" regarding the fees he was continuing to levy on investors sat in his fund.

But it wouldn't be long before Bailey and the FCA would also come under intense scrutiny for their own failures to spot some of the early warning signs that could have prevented the Woodford disaster from unfolding.

III

Andrew Bailey and FCA chairman Charles Randall entered Portcullis House opposite the Houses of Parliament braced for a grilling from Morgan and other MPs on the Treasury select committee.

Bailey was no stranger to attending the formal sessions with MPs, but on this occasion the stakes were particularly high. By the time of his appearance in front of the Treasury Select committee on 25 June 2019, Bailey was already one of the bookmaker's favourites to succeed Mark Carney as Bank of England governor. The Treasury and other senior government officials would be closely watching his performance in front of MPs in what was an unofficial interview for the top job.

As the grilling got underway, Conservative MPs Steve Baker and Simon Clarke declared from the outset they were both investors in Woodford's fund, and that both were clients of Hargreaves Lansdown. This was likely to be an uncomfortable ride for Bailey.

Morgan had already been in touch with Bailey by letter the week after Woodford's fund was suspended, demanding answers about the FCA's communication between Link and the authorities in Guernsey regarding Woodford's move to list some of his unquoted holdings. Morgan claimed the FCA should have spotted these sooner, after Bailey admitted the regulator only became aware of them when they were revealed in a *Citywire* article three months earlier.

"My comment was 'does anyone in the FCA read the newspapers?'," says Morgan. "People look at these things but they don't often ask what might be going on and whether it should be looked into."

Morgan had a point. The FCA had been in regular contact with Link since 2017, when it had asked it to stop valuing Woodford's unlisted assets itself and ensure it had in place an independent third party to carry out the valuations. Some of Woodford's unquoted holdings experienced huge valuation increases, such as Industrial Heat which rose by 357% in September 2018. Benevolent AI also saw its valuation hiked over the period Woodford held it, up around 600% from when he first invested.[68]

The regulator was again in touch with Link in February 2018 after Woodford's fund first breached the regulatory limit for unquoted holdings, and it was being provided with monthly reports on its liquidity position.

Bailey had told Morgan in a written response to her letter that the FCA had opened an investigation into the events leading up to Woodford's fund suspension. But questions were being asked why the FCA failed to spot the red flags sooner.

Bailey instead tried to shift blame to a "flaw" in the EU rules governing Woodford's fund, which did not require Link to notify the FCA about the Guernsey listing. He admitted that Woodford's fund was "sailing close to the wind" and that it had pushed the regulations to the very limit, suggesting it was not within the spirit of the rules. But Bailey was adamant there was no failure regarding the FCA's supervision. "I do think it's more a failure of rules, that's my view," he told the committee.

Bailey was not the only high-profile figure to cast doubt over whether Woodford's fund was fully adhering to EU rules. Bank of England governor Mark Carney went much further during his appearance before the select committee a day later. By coincidence, the issue of fund liquidity was in the news the same week after an investment company called H2O Asset Management experienced billions of euros in investor withdrawals from a range of its funds following concerns about illiquid bonds held with a controversial German financier, Lars Windhorst.

The smooth-talking Canadian was careful not to mention Woodford's fund by name, but it was absolutely clear his comments about fund liquidity were directed at the suspended fund. "This is a big deal. You can see something that could be systemic," Carney told the select committee. "These funds are built on a lie, which is that you can have daily liquidity for assets that fundamentally aren't liquid. And that leads to an expectation of individuals that it's not that different to having money in a bank."

Woodford was now seriously struggling to save his Equity Income fund. The contagion had started to spread to the Patient Capital trust, as some of the companies Woodford was looking to offload were held across both funds. Between the Equity Income fund announcing its suspension to the end of July, the trust's share price plummeted by 38%. The situation worsened after the board of Patient Capital revealed that Woodford had sold about 60% of his personal stake in the trust, worth around £1m, to pay a personal tax bill. Woodford said he was a "reluctant seller" of the large stake, but had kept it quiet for three weeks before notifying board members about it.

Woodford was starting to look incredibly vulnerable. Sensing his possible demise, rival fund managers started to sniff out an opportunity. Several City fund managers had approached the trust's board to offer their services, should they decide to give struggling Woodford the boot. For the time being, the board said it was keeping its options open.

Remarkably, Woodford clung on.

Just a month after the suspension, the impact was being acutely felt by those working at the office in Oxford. Fees were still coming through the door, but the crisis prompted Woodford and Newman to inform around 45 staff what they already sensed was coming: redundancies were now almost certain.

11

Trampled Under Foot

The 4pm sacking

I

O N Monday 14 October, Woodford and Newman travelled from Oxford to Link's headquarters in London for a 4pm crunch meeting with Karl Midl. It was an encounter that would seal Woodford's fate.

Communication between Link and Woodford had become less frequent in recent weeks, save for a brief update at the end of September where Woodford said he was on track to sell the fund's most problematic assets and reposition the portfolio towards more liquid companies. As far as Woodford was concerned, everything was going to plan and the meeting at Link's offices in the City was a formality – merely a chance to provide the information Link needed to update the FCA on the progress made.

Woodford had been working flat out since the suspension to get the fund's portfolio into shape, shifting its exposure away from the most illiquid companies that had landed it in so much trouble. By the time the meeting with Link took place, more than 80% of the cash raised from selling stakes in less liquid companies had been reinvested in some of the UK's largest firms, such as British American Tobacco, BT and IAG.

The weekend before meeting Midl, Woodford and his team had thrashed out a presentation that would outline the biggest changes made to the portfolio since the suspension, notably how cash levels had been raised in the fund to cushion investor redemptions when it reopened. The presentation would also detail how stakes among some of the harder to sell companies had been reduced from 34% to 23%.

Woodford was not naive. He knew Link had the option to wind down the fund at any moment. But he planned to argue that it would be the most detrimental approach for investors. Other options, such as a longer suspension period or continuing to reposition the portfolio, should be on the table. Woodford believed that Link should not assume all investors in the fund wanted to redeem their investment.

Woodford was still working on the basis that the fund would re-open in December, and a series of roadshows had been planned over the next couple of months to showcase some of the changes that had been made. The roadshows would be an opportunity for Woodford to present an overhauled fund to the army of financial advisers who had recommended Equity

Income to their clients, as well as gauge the level of outflows that could be expected when the suspension lifted.

Woodford was in no doubt that hundreds of millions of pounds would exit immediately when the gates were opened, including Kent County Council's multi-million-pound holding. But some investment professionals expected around £600m to remain in the fund after the most jittery investors had cut their losses once the suspension was lifted.

Woodford was never given the opportunity to give his presentation to Link.

———————

As he and Newman sat around the meeting table to talk about their approach with the fund, Midl dealt the final blow. It left Woodford and Newman dumbfounded. Link had decided to wind down Equity Income and return money to investors. It had always been the nuclear option – but Woodford and Newman never thought it would be taken.

The process of liquidating the fund would mean sacking Woodford. The fund he had spent five years building from scratch was now taken from his grasp. There was no point Woodford and Newman trying to argue their case with Link. The decision was final.

After the hour-long meeting, Woodford and Newman emerged onto Gresham Street – a short distance from the Bank of England – in complete bewilderment, thoughts scrambling around their heads about what they would do next and whether the business would be able to survive.

It would almost certainly create another media firestorm when the story broke.

The following morning, an announcement was emailed from Link to investors. At odds with what Woodford believed, Link said that opening the fund in December was no longer achievable. "Whilst progress has been made in relation to repositioning the fund's assets, this has unfortunately not been sufficient to allow reasonable certainty as to when the repositioning would be fully achieved and the fund could be re-opened," Link said in its statement.

The wind-up process would see remaining assets in the fund split into two parts – one comprised of listed stocks that would be easy to offload and the other made up of unlisted and highly illiquid shares. Link appointed BlackRock, a New York-headquartered asset manager, to handle the sale of the most liquid companies. PJT Partners was put in place to offload the illiquid portion.

The decision to oust him angered Woodford, who issued a terse one-sentence response to Link's statement. "This was Link's decision and one I cannot accept, nor believe is in the long-term interests of Woodford Equity Income fund investors," he said.

Without Equity Income, which since the suspension had provided millions of pounds in revenues, time was running out for Woodford to consider his next move.

II

On the evening of 15 October 2019, business journalists from some of Britain's most prestigious news outlets were starting to gather in a private dining room above the exclusive Ivy restaurant in Covent Garden.

Organised by Fidelity International, one of the City's largest asset managers, the event was supposed to be an opportunity for finance hacks to mingle with the company's top brass and quiz them on investment matters such as the escalating trade war between the US and China and the UK's impending exit from the European Union.

But for the hacks and investment professionals propping up the art deco style bar in the centre of the room, there was one only topic being discussed that evening: Neil Woodford.

Journalists were only too happy for the excuse to unwind with a few drinks, having spent much of the day chasing industry contacts for reaction to Woodford's sacking. As a few latecomers began to bottleneck by the dining room's narrow doorway at the top of the stairs, it became clear what had been holding them up. There was to be one final twist in the Woodford story.

Less than 12 hours after announcing that Link had sacked him as manager of Equity Income, Woodford handed in his resignation from the remaining funds he managed. It was all over.

An email dropped into the inboxes of journalists just as they were about to sit down for dinner. It was from Roland Cross, a veteran public relations executive who had been helping Woodford's team manage communications during the ongoing crisis. "We have taken the highly painful decision to close Woodford Investment Management," Woodford said in a short statement. "I personally deeply regret the impact events have had on individuals who placed their faith in Woodford Investment Management and invested in our funds."

Given the dramatic turn of events, it was a brief comment from a fund manager whose more than two-decade career had come crashing down. It was to be the last public statement that Woodford would make.

The sun had not yet risen on Garsington Road when Woodford Investment Management staff began to arrive on 16 October for one-to-one meetings with Yvonne Pownall, the company's head of HR.

"We all knew what was going to happen," says one of the employees.

The business had already cut ties with the bulk of its contractors over the previous months. A majority of the employees left behind were now dismissed immediately. Those who had previously been told to work notice periods remained at home. Only others in more senior roles stayed on to help see the business to its natural end.

It was a brutal end to a turbulent four months for Woodford's loyal workforce, who had stuck by their boss and worked long days to try and salvage the business. Woodford's employees were in shock just as much as their boss about his rapid downfall. Some were angry with Link's decision and thought Woodford should have been given until the end of the year to work on the portfolio.

"What was really shocking was Link decided to flip the switch almost randomly," says the former employee. "If Neil had failed to deliver by the end of the year, what they did may have been more appropriate. What's happened to the fund since demonstrates it has done nobody any favours. Neil was killing himself to get the fund open again."

After Woodford handed in his notice, Link announced that Income Focus, his only remaining fund, would also be suspended. Outflows from that fund had stabilised in the weeks leading up to Woodford's decision to quit, but Link could not risk a situation where anxious investors would exit en masse, particularly as a large proportion of assets were illiquid holdings.

While Link figured out what to do next, another cohort of Woodford investors were now trapped and faced an anxious wait.

Woodford would work his three-month notice period as manager of the Patient Capital trust, which saw its share price hit a new low as investors were caught up in the panic and decided to cash out. The board of the Patient Capital trust, which had just a few months previously acknowledged it was in talks with other fund managers, now had to accelerate plans to find a replacement.

III

Woodford's demise had been inconceivable when he struck out on his own in 2014.

Six years to the day since announcing his departure from Invesco, Woodford found himself amid the smouldering remains of the empire he had left to create. The career of Britain's best-known fund manager was over, his reputation damaged beyond repair.

Woodford had been treading water for four months, but even some market pundits who predicted he would struggle to pull through were taken aback by how quickly everything came to an end.

There were limited options for Woodford, who as well as a star fund manager had also been one of the biggest brands in the business. "The brand damage was so great it would have cast a long shadow over anything else he would have done in the retail market," says Ryan Hughes, head of active portfolios at investment platform AJ Bell. "It will make people think twice about putting blind faith in somebody. And it will also make people think hard about the concept of the 'star' investor."

Link spent the next two months after the collapse of Woodford's business sifting through the wreckage and working through a plan for his Income Focus fund, which had by now shrunk to £253m, down by more than 65% since its peak a year earlier. Aberdeen Standard Investments, the fund manager Hargreaves Lansdown had worked with to try and throw a lifeline to Equity Income, was announced as the new manager of the Income Focus fund in December.

When the fund re-opened in February 2020, its new managers Charles Luke and Thomas Moore had given the portfolio a complete makeover. Only two of Woodford's top ten holdings remained. Meanwhile the board of the Patient Capital trust appointed Schroders to pick up the mandate.

Some of those who worked closely with Woodford took pity on him. "For a number of people it was the end of the road," says one employee. "The press seemed to be producing this narrative that he was a kind of Bond villain. The reality is that there was no malice in the way the fund was managed. A number of judgement calls just turned out to be the wrong ones.

"Because the portfolio was fragile and illiquid, what would normally be a cyclical lull in performance precipitated a negative spiral. Fund managers experience poor performance all the time. It just doesn't culminate in a national scandal."

Those who knew Woodford from earlier in his career were also in disbelief. The promising young upstart they had watched go on to become the UK's most successful fund manager was now a byword for arrogant speculation. His fund management firm had made him, and a small circle of confidants, very rich. Everyone else who had trusted him had lost money.

"I followed him and put some of my own money with him," says Ian Marshall, Woodford's old boss from his days at TSB. "He was trying to duplicate the same success in two different investment styles. But it's difficult. I didn't know him as an arrogant person, but perhaps it was intellectual arrogance that he could do it again.

"He seemed to handle it badly. I was disappointed about the fee aspect. I knew him as an honourable, hard-working person. I was sad that he didn't act as I think he is – an honourable man."

12

How Many More Times

The fallout

I

MARK BARNETT had been fighting for five years to try and plug the constant flow of money leaving the two flagship funds he had taken over from Woodford at Invesco.

The father of four had inherited a tough gig when he was handed the reins in 2014, made harder by the fact he was unable to shake off the connection with his former colleague. For years after Woodford's exit from Henley-on-Thames, Barnett continued to be described by the media as his protégé. His performance was consistently scrutinised and compared to that of his predecessor.

It was easy to see why.

Barnett had largely stuck to the same investment approach

as Woodford. His funds even continued to hold investments in some of the smaller, less liquid companies Woodford had picked before departing. There were other similarities, including some of those companies which delivered disastrous results, such as Provident Financial.

No sooner had Woodford's business empire imploded, than Barnett found himself facing a mounting crisis of his own. Investors began to question whether he was doomed to fall victim to the same liquidity problems. At Invesco's Henley office, the situation rapidly deteriorated once Woodford's empire came crashing down.

Woodford had spent the past four months under the spotlight as he grappled to save his flagship fund. Now all eyes were on Barnett.

A little over three weeks after Woodford's shock announcement to shutter his business, Barnett's Income and High Income funds were hit with a downgrade by Morningstar. Peter Brunt, the Morningstar analyst who had heavily criticised Woodford's Equity Income fund when his firm made the same downgrade decision, cited concerns about Barnett's "sizeable overweight" positions in smaller companies.

By the end of September 2019, small and micro-cap companies accounted for 30% of assets in Barnett's funds. Analysts were starting to worry that he could struggle to continue meeting investor withdrawals given the high exposure his funds had to companies that were difficult to sell. "While the group has been able to meet redemptions so far, Barnett's continued intent on investing in smaller names gives us cause for concern," Brunt said at the time.[69]

Barnett was also battling severe performance issues. The High Income fund had returned 0.8% over the year to when Morningstar downgraded it, around 10.8% behind the average performance of a comparable fund in the same sector. Over a five-year period, it had returned 2%, about 3.7% behind its category average.

The funds' assets had also dwindled at an alarming rate. High Income managed £13.1bn when Barnett took it over from Woodford, shrinking to £6.1bn five years later. The Income fund had not fared much better, with assets of £2.7bn by November 2019 down from £8.3bn when Barnett was handed control.

The downgrade from Morningstar was the final straw – Barnett had to distance himself from Woodford once and for all. The following day Barnett penned a note to his investors in an attempt to play down the concerns raised by Morningstar, telling them any comparisons made to Woodford were "misplaced".[70]

"My funds are appropriately positioned, well diversified and able to generate liquidity should investors wish to buy or sell," he said in the note, pointing to the fact he had reduced exposure to unquoted companies by around £500m in the five years he had managed them. "The events at [Woodford Investment Management] have understandably drawn much comment from investors, the media and the wider market. Given that Neil Woodford worked at Invesco and previously managed these portfolios, questions of comparison are perhaps inevitable. However, under my stewardship the funds have chartered a very different course and it cannot be overstated that the portfolios I manage are very different."

Barnett claimed the overlap between his funds and those managed by Woodford at his new venture was less than 15%. In what could be interpreted as a shot at Woodford, Barnett said he was subject to strict compliance and risk oversight and an experienced senior management team – some of the factors that had led Woodford to seek a new course away from Invesco.

"I am supported to make independent investment decisions, yes, but I am also accountable and well challenged," Barnett said.

It was not enough to reassure investors.

The following month Barnett was sacked as the manager of the Edinburgh Investment Trust. He had taken over managing the trust from Woodford in 2014, but more than three years of underperformance had sealed his fate.

Zurich, a pensions provider, also dealt a blow to Barnett by pulling his two flagship funds from those it offered to customers. It said the ongoing reduction in the size of the funds and concerns about Barnett's ability to manage liquidity were the main reasons behind its decision.

Then, in April, the board of the Perpetual Income and Growth Investment Trust dropped Barnett as its manager after more than two decades in the role. The board had voiced its concerns on several occasions about poor performance, claiming it gave Barnett enough time to turn things around. But with the trust's share price having fallen by 50% over five years, it had decided to begin the search for a new manager.

Ultimately the heavy outflows were too much for Invesco to bear any longer. In May 2020 the company announced that Barnett would depart after a 24-year tenure.

II

The FCA has not come out of the Woodford debacle well.

More than a year after it announced it had launched an investigation into the events leading up to the suspension of Equity Income, investors are still waiting for answers and any signs that lessons have been learned.

To some, the FCA were simply asleep at the wheel and failed to spot the warning signs when Woodford strayed into illiquid holdings and the fund morphed into something far riskier than investors had been led to believe.

The regulator has attracted fierce criticism from some of the City's heaviest hitters, including Paul Myners, a former fund management chief executive and ex-City minister in Gordon Brown's Labour government.

"In the background we have the FCA who look like the people in white suits in *Line of Duty*, the scene-of-crime inspectors, who arrive after the damage has been done and did not anticipate what was happening," he told the BBC shortly after the fund was suspended.[71]

"The people losing out here are the end investors. The professionals are OK, the regulator will give itself two years to carry out a review of what went wrong, and the same risks will continue of allowing illiquid assets to be put in portfolios that are treated as if they are liquid."

Link has also come under fire for the way it handled the wind-up of Woodford's largest fund, with accusations that it sold off assets at fire-sale prices. In the month following the suspension, boutique bank WG Partners was given exclusivity to scour the market for a group of investors to buy a portfolio of biotech companies Woodford had built up in Equity Income.

WG Partners had until the end of January to finalise a sale, but failed to find any investors willing to purchase the assets by the deadline. This posed a potential opportunity for Woodford, who began to meet with a small number of investors and City contacts to discuss the possibility of snapping up the companies himself.

The meetings came to nothing. In June 2020 Link announced an agreement had been reached with Acacia Research Corporation, a US-based company, to sell around 19 healthcare companies owned by Equity Income for £244m. Questions were immediately raised about the low valuations slapped on some of these companies, after it emerged that Acacia netted a $27m profit on one holding it picked up.[72]

Research from *Citywire* showed that Acacia bought holdings in Evofem Biosciences for $2.1m before selling the shares later the same day for $29.3m. Acacia's sale of Midatech Pharma, which was acquired from Woodford's fund, generated a profit of £750,000.

Acacia's chief executive later dismissed the criticism as "silly". "There was one single price given, which we agreed for the entire portfolio," he told the *Sunday Times*.[73]

Scrutiny over Link's actions intensified after an investigation carried out by the newspaper revealed investors in Equity Income had seen the value of assets plummet by £1bn in the year since the fund was suspended.[74]

Payouts to investors who were trapped in Equity Income are still ongoing. Savers locked in Equity Income received their first payments in January 2020, six months after the fund was suspended, when it emerged that BlackRock had raised around £1.9bn from the sale of the fund's most liquid holdings.

By the time this book is printed, investors will have received payments totalling almost £2.5bn. But they face a long wait to receive the full amounts they are entitled to. Link said offloading the remaining illiquid assets held by the fund – some £290m worth – could take until late 2021.

Winding up the fund has created a lucrative revenue stream for those involved. According to the annual report and accounts for Equity Income, BlackRock was paid close to £10m for its role in offloading the assets in the fund. A further £3.2m was paid to PJT Park Hill, while Debevoise & Plimpton, which provided specialist legal support to assist with the sale of unquoted assets, received £2.5m.[75]

III

Woodford's downfall occurred at a time when British fund managers were already grappling with severe reputational issues. A landmark study by the FCA in 2017 concluded that most of them failed to deliver performance in line with the fees they charge, and that the investment management sector was plagued by a lack of competition, enabling it to earn some of the highest profit margins in the UK economy.[76]

Given the continuous run of poor performance – the majority of stock pickers have failed to beat index trackers over the past decade – investors had already been turning their backs on expensive funds in favour of cheaper passive investments which track major indices, like the FTSE 100 or S&P 500.[77]

Woodford's fall from grace did not help matters.

During 2019 investment funds managed by stock pickers posted withdrawals of £32bn, with Morningstar citing "black marks" on the industry, like Woodford's downfall, doing little to stem the flow to passive funds.[78]

Some are worried Woodford's demise has further dangerously eroded confidence in the UK's fund management industry, at a time when savers are being encouraged to put more money into the stock market to prepare for their futures. "Woodford was sold as a safe, marketable, daily-priced investment fund. He ended up investing in things that weren't daily priced," says Baroness Ros Altmann, a former pensions minister in David Cameron's Conservative government. "It is worrying that we have one of the darlings of the retail industry not only having failed, but it looks as if the interests of consumers have been playing second fiddle to the interests of this fund manager who people totally trusted."

Lawyers have been quick to pounce on a potential litigation opportunity emerging from the scandal, and have already received thousands of enquiries from Woodford investors who want the fund manager, Hargreaves Lansdown and Link to face up to their actions.

Harcus Parker, one of the law firms involved, has sent a pre-action letter to Link on behalf of 8,000 investors – the first stage in the litigation process. There is history between the two sides. The law firm reached an out-of-court settlement with Link's predecessor, Capita Financial Managers, over its handling of the collapsed Arch Cru funds in 2015. At least two other law firms are eyeing up potential cases.

Whatever the outcome of any legal challenges the various actors in this long-running saga may face, one thing is certain: Woodford is unlikely to be welcomed back by UK investors anytime soon. The reputational damage caused by the implosion of his business is too severe to contemplate him ever managing money on behalf of retail savers again.

For now, Woodford has been keeping a low profile. But there have been some suggestions he is trying to manoeuvre his way back into fund management in some form. Reports emerged in December 2019 that he and Newman had jetted off to China to gauge interest among local investors about investing in early-stage companies.[79] A similar excursion was also completed to the Middle East, but the exploratory talks have so far amounted to nothing.

More recently, the pair were linked with Juno Capital, a boutique investment firm which was considering snapping up some of the assets in Equity Income. Juno was later forced to issue a statement denying that Woodford and Newman were joining as employees, stating that talks had merely taken place to access their knowledge and expertise.

Investors will have lost out, but Woodford is likely to be financially comfortable for the rest of his life. Accounts for Woodford Investment Management in the year to the end of March 2019 – three months before Equity Income was suspended – revealed that he and Newman had paid themselves around £13.8m in dividends with the business on the verge of crisis and when investors had already started pulling money.

It brought the total amount the pair earned to £111.5m since founding the firm in 2014 – a reminder of the personal wealth they generated during the time they were in business together.

Time will tell whether some of Woodford's more controversial holdings would have come good, and if he should have been given until the end of 2019 to overhaul the portfolio. At least one of his holdings, UK-based biotech company Synairgen, has caught the attention of former Woodford investors. The AIM-listed company's share price rose 420% in one day in July 2020 after it announced the results of trials for a drug to treat coronavirus patients. The stock was among those sold off to Acacia Research for a knock-down price several weeks earlier, meaning Woodford investors felt none of the benefit from the share price's meteoric rise.

Another key Woodford investment, Oxford Nanopore, announced in October 2020 it had raised more than £84m in fresh capital from investors. The biotech company has been one of those at the forefront of developing rapid turnaround Covid tests.

Much has been written about how much Woodford himself was responsible for his own demise. While his shift in investment style contributed to some of the difficulties his blockbuster fund encountered, it would be wrong to pin the blame on one individual.

"As with RBS and Fred Goodwin, there was a complex cocktail of environment and individual hubris and arrogance," says Colin Mclean, a fund manager and chief executive of SVM Asset Management. "The whole promotion of the fund was presented as a large-scale, low-cost opportunity for investors, when there should have been much more concern about scalability."

In an interview with the *Daily Telegraph* ahead of the launch of his new business in 2014, Woodford outlined how he believed himself to be a better fund manager given his 26 years' experience and that he expected to be around for decades to come. "It's no surprise to me that one of the world's best investors – Warren Buffett – is also one of the oldest," Woodford said in the interview. "But fund managers tend to move jobs frequently and quit the industry early, which means that the lessons they learn are often forgotten."[80]

Woodford has been forced out of the industry earlier than

he planned, his grand plan to conquer the UK retail fund management market under his own steam falling flat with dramatic consequences.

Whether Woodford can salvage his reputation from the wreckage left behind after the implosion of his business remains to be seen. But the hundreds of thousands of investors who were locked in his fund will be hoping lessons will be learned from this scandal, and that they are not the ones who are forgotten.

A NOTE ON SOURCES

The bulk of material included in *When the Fund Stops* originates from extensive interviews conducted with former colleagues of Neil Woodford, those who have worked with him at various points during a career which started in the early 1980s.

Due to the sensitive nature of the topic, most interviews were carried out on the basis that individuals would not be identified, allowing them to speak more freely and for their quotes to play a vital role in telling the untold story of Woodford's rise and fall. Despite their anonymity, their comments have not been exaggerated for effect.

There were many knockbacks along the way. Not all former colleagues of Woodford's were willing to speak to me – some suggested there was nothing more to explore in the story of his downfall. I hope this book proves them wrong.

Writing about Woodford's earlier life and career would not have been possible without the input of Jo Woodford, who I spoke to at length during my research. She provided valuable details about her former husband's life before he made a name for himself as one of Britain's best-known fund managers.

Delving into the archives of the *Maidenhead Advertiser* also helped uncover stories about Woodford's sporting achievements as a schoolboy.

Correspondence sent to the Treasury Committee by Andrew Bailey and Christopher Hill formed part of my research into the roles played by the Financial Conduct Authority and Hargreaves Lansdown in the run-up to the suspension of the Equity Income fund. These are documents made available to the public.

Alongside my own research, I benefited from some of the extensive reporting carried out by fellow financial journalists who have covered Woodford's career so diligently over many years. Where I have included information from their articles, this is cited in the notes.

The ultimate goal in writing this book was to present a fair, balanced representation of events leading up to the collapse of Woodford's business in October 2019.

The final manuscript was not seen by Woodford. I hope one day he will be ready to tell his side of the story. When he is, I will be ready to listen.

ACKNOWLEDGEMENTS

Writing a book is no easy feat. But I was incredibly fortunate to have input and support from countless sources who spoke to me for this book on condition of anonymity. You know who you are and I'm extremely grateful you gave up your valuable time to help with my research, often fielding questions and phone calls from me on multiple occasions.

I would particularly like to thank Jo Woodford for her considerable contribution and for telling me her story. To Ian Marshall, Graham Walden and Nick Stein – thank you for casting your minds back many decades to recall what it was like to know Neil Woodford before he went on to make his mark in the world of fund management. I'm also grateful to Gavin Coventry, a former teacher at Maidenhead Grammar School, for sharing information about Woodford's sporting prowess.

To the investors who entrusted large amounts of their savings with Neil Woodford and are still waiting for answers – and payments – thank you for allowing me to include your experiences in this book. I'm also grateful to retirement coach Richard Cook for his help on this front.

Baroness Nicky Morgan and John Chatfeild-Roberts were also kind enough to provide their insights.

A huge thanks to Christopher Parker at Harriman House, who first approached me after seeing the potential in a book about Neil Woodford's downfall. His boundless enthusiasm made the entire process of writing my first book pain-free, and I'm grateful for his suggestions on how to improve my original manuscript.

Professor Amin Rajan was also a valuable sounding board.

I'd also like to thank Shruti Tripathi Chopra, Trista Kelley and Francesco Guerrera at *Financial News* for giving this book their blessing and allowing me the time off work over the summer to research and begin writing.

But my biggest thanks goes to my wife, Tara. She had never heard of Neil Woodford, but is now something of an authority on his life and career as this book became the main talking point over the kitchen table while I was writing it.

Often there were times when I wondered if I'd ever achieve the end goal, but she kept me going with words of encouragement, hugs, coffee and unwavering support. I simply couldn't have done it without her.

ENDNOTES

1   'Neil Woodford talks: "My best is still to come"', Richard Evans, *Daily Telegraph*, 3 May 2014

2   www.hl.co.uk/news/articles/archive/cf-woodford-equity-income-one-year-anniversary

3   'Neil Woodford: The man who can't stop making money', Brian Milligan, BBC News website, 18 June 2015

4   Source: KCC pension fund accounts and KCC spokesperson. Value of investment at 31.3.2017 was £316,607,000. Value of investment at fund suspension on 03.06.2019 was £237.6m.

5   'For investors looking for a stairway to heaven, one man is out in front', Miles Costello, *The Times*, 7 February 2015

6   Birth and marriage records

7   ' There's no science to investing, just be arrogant – and humble', Aimee Donnellan, *The Sunday Times*, 11 October 2015

8   *Maidenhead Advertiser*, 19 February 1971

9   *Maidenhead Advertiser*, 25 November 1977

10   'Why Britain's top fund guru Neil Woodford is buying shares when everyone else is selling', Holly Black, *Daily Mail*, 14 October 2015

11   Ibid

12   www.lloydsbankinggroup.com/who-we-are/our-heritage/timeline.html

13   Will of Victor Woodford

14   'Era ends as Hill Samuel loses its deal-makers', Peter Rodgers, *The Independent*, 1 June 1996

15   'A Perpetual talent for winning', James Bethell, *The Sunday Times*, 25 September 1994

16   'Snurge is retired', *The Independent*, 19 October 1994

17   'How the rich grew richer in 1993', Philip Beresford, Matthew Lynn, Kirstie Hamilton, *The Sunday Times*, 26 December 1993

18   *In for a Penny: A Business Adventure*, Peter Hargreaves, 2009

19   'Order a Pizza Through Dreamcast', IGN Staff, ign.com, 10 December 1999 (www.ign.com/articles/1999/12/10/order-a-pizza-through-dreamcast)

20   'Don't gamble on big three', Jeff Prestridge, *Mail on Sunday*, 13 March 2000

21 'The dotcom bubble 20 years on: "It felt like the gold rush"', James Titcomb, Olivia Rudgard and Laurence Dodds, *Daily Telegraph*, 10 March 2020

22 'AstraZeneca boss David Brennan quits under pressure from investors', Julia Kollewe, *The Guardian*, 26 April 2012

23 'Boardroom coup at haulier Stobart Group', Mark Wembridge, *Financial Times*, 21 January 2013

24 'Investor ire over BAE', David Oakley, *Financial Times*, 21 September 2012

25 Ibid

26 'Woodford: industry is failing on corporate engagement', Emma Dunkley, *Citywire*, 5 March 2013

27 'Esso tiger fuels planning row', BBC News, 28 September 1998

28 'Invesco Perpetual fined £18.6m for failings in fund management', FCA press release, 28 April 2014

29 'Invesco's Barnett aims to build on Woodford's long-term legacy', Mike Foster, *Financial News*, 18 October 2013

30 'Anthony Bolton: "I was wrong about China"', Bradley Gerrard, *Investment Adviser*, 7 April 2014

31 'Key person risk lessens as star fund managers fade', David Ricketts, *Financial Times*, 14 March 2016.

32 Data from Morningstar Direct

33 'Porsches, horses… and £6m lair like a Bond villain: Guy Adams investigates Neil Woodford, the investment fund chief who has stopped savers from withdrawing their own cash', *Daily Mail*, 13 June 2019

34 'Paxman in planning row over "unsightly" equestrian centre', Anita Singh, *The Telegraph*, 17 September 2011

35 'Oakley Capital: The firm behind Woodford's new venture', Nick Reeve, *Investment Adviser*, 19 December 2013

36 'Unquoteds have huge potential', Neil Woodford, *Investors Chronicle*, 21 November 2014

37 'The five biggest trust launches of all time (apart from Woodford's): Where are they now?', Daniel Lanyon, Trustnet.com, 21 April 2015

38 'Woodford Income Focus – portfolio revealed', Hargreaves Lansdown website, 17 May 2017

39 'Porsches, horses… and £6m lair like a Bond villain: Guy Adams investigates Neil Woodford, the investment fund chief who has stopped savers from withdrawing their own cash', *Daily Mail*, 13 June 2019

40 *Sunday Times* 2020 Rich List

41 'Peter Hargreaves, the modest multimillionaire', Richard Wachman, *The Guardian*, 30 June 2011

42 *In for a Penny: A Business Adventure*, Peter Hargreaves, 2009

43 *Effective Investing: A simple way to build wealth by investing in funds*, Mark Dampier, 2015

44 Hargreaves Lansdown letter to Treasury Committee chair, 18 June 2019

45 www.fca.org.uk/publication/occasional-papers/occasional-paper-30.pdf

46 'A follow up with Neil Woodford', Hargreaves Lansdown website, 9 January 2018

47 Peter Hargreaves: Neil Woodford 'did not tell the truth', Peter Evans, *Sunday Times*, 22 September 2019

48 *Effective Investing: A simple way to build wealth by investing in funds*, Mark Dampier, 2015

49 'Bad "cold fusion" investment contributed to Woodford fund collapse', Steven Krivit, *New Energy Times*, 7 June 2019

50 *An Impossible Invention: The True Story of the Energy Source that Could Change the World*, Mats Lewan, 2014

51 'The long shot science that attracted Brad Pitt and Neil Woodford', Kadhim Shubber, Robert Smith, Peter Smith, *Financial Times*, 14 June 2019

52 Email provided in court documents

53 'The longtime links between Neil Woodford and a City broking minnow', Cat Rutter Pooley, *Financial Times*, 28 June 2019

54   Employment tribunal judgment, N Malik v Cenkos
Securities, 17 January 2018

55   www.fca.org.uk/publication/final-notices/capita-
financial-managers-limited-2017.pdf

56   www.linkassetservices.com/news/sale-of-capita-asset-
services-to-link-group-for-888-million

57   Woodford Equity Income fund portfolio update, 3 May
2019

58   Neil Woodford blog: update on Provident Financial,
22 August 2017

59   'Neil Woodford: Will investors keep the faith?' Claer
Barrett and Kate Beioley, *Financial Times*, 1 December 2017

60   'Woodford accuses critics of misleading investors', Peter
Smith and Kate Beioley, *Financial Times*, 14 March 2019

61   Kent County Council Superannuation Fund report and
accounts

62   Woodford Equity Income fund factsheet, 31 May 2019

63   'Woodford feels heat as St James's steps up scrutiny', Kate
Beioley, *Financial Times*, 24 May 2019

64   Andrew Bailey appearance on Bloomberg Surveillance,
5 June 2019

65   'Craig Newman: the silent CEO at the centre of the
Woodford crisis', David Ricketts, *Financial News*, 24 June 2019

66 'Boss of stricken Woodford fund secretly sells £15m of property', David Byers, *The Times*, 2 August 2019

67 'Woodford amasses £7.5m as fund freeze hits four months', Chris Newlands and Samuel Agini, *Financial News*, 30 September 2019

68 'Link feels heat over valuation of Woodford's unquoted stocks', Daniel Grote, *Citywire*, 19 June 2019

69 'Mark Barnett funds downgraded on small-cap concerns', Morningstar, 7 November 2019

70 Note sent to investors from Mark Barnett on 9 November 2019

71 'City watchdog "missed Neil Woodford fund warning signs"', BBC News online, 7 June 2019 (www.bbc.com/news/business-48552660)

72 'Revealed: Buyer's $27m profit from cut-price Woodford stock', Daniel Grote, *Citywire*, 24 July 2020

73 'Acacia Research defends swoop on Neil Woodford's biotech babies', Sabah Meddings, *Sunday Times*, 21 June 2020

74 'Woodford: £1bn lost in a year', Ali Hussain, *Sunday Times*, 26 July 2020

75 Equity Income annual report and accounts from 1 January 2019 to 31 March 2020

76 FCA Asset Management Market Study, June 2017

77 'Active fund performance worsens further, says Morningstar', David Ricketts, *Financial News*, 10 September 2019

78 '"Black marks" for stockpickers help passive gains in 2019', David Ricketts, *Financial News*, 24 January 2020

79 'Spurned in Britain, Woodford heads to China for his next act', Suzy Waite and Lucca De Paoli, *Bloomberg*, 18 December 2019

80 'Neil Woodford talks: "My best is still to come"', Richard Evans, *Daily Telegraph*, 3 May 2014

INDEX

Y

Yerbury, Bob 46–7

Z

Zurich 168